WORLD KITCHEN

THAILAND

WORLD KITCHEN

THAILAND

MURDOCH BOOKS

Contents

INTRODUCTION ❊❊❊ 7

SNACKS AND STREET FOOD ❊❊❊ 12
FOOD JOURNEY: STREET FOOD ❊❊❊ 30

SOUPS ❊❊❊ 46

SALADS ❊❊❊ 66
FOOD JOURNEY: FRUIT ❊❊❊ 78

FISH AND SHELLFISH ❊❊❊ 86
FOOD JOURNEY: FISH AND SEAFOOD ❊❊❊ 96

MEAT AND POULTRY ❊❊❊ 108

CURRIES ❊❊❊ 124
FOOD JOURNEY: FLAVOURINGS ❊❊❊ 142

STIR-FRIES ❊❊❊ 152

NOODLES AND RICE ❊❊❊ 174
FOOD JOURNEY: RICE ❊❊❊ 194

VEGETABLES ❊❊❊ 200

DESSERTS ❊❊❊ 216
FOOD JOURNEY: SWEETS ❊❊❊ 228

BASICS ❊❊❊ 234
GLOSSARY ❊❊❊ 248
INDEX ❊❊❊ 253

THAILAND, FOR CENTURIES A STOP-OFF FOR TRADERS, HAS SKILFULLY ASSIMILATED INFLUENCES FROM OTHER COUNTRIES INTO ITS OWN DISTINCTIVE CUISINE WITHOUT COMPROMISING LOCAL CULTURE AND RITUALS.

Despite acting as a trade conduit throughout its history, Thailand, unlike many other Asian nations, has never been ruled by a European power. Mystical and exotic, Siam, as Thailand was once known, managed simultaneously to charm, manipulate and resist her European visitors. Closer neighbours were not so easily rebuffed and Thailand was periodically invaded, most notably by Burma. Despite these incursions, Thailand's remarkably stable religious (Buddhist) and cultural history, coupled with an abundance of locally grown food, is reflected in its historic cuisine.

Most Thai men spend at least three months of their young lives as a monk and, since monks are fed by everyone in the community as a mark of respect, so food and religion are bound together. The basic tenets of Thai cuisine are ancient in origin and they were upheld for centuries by the royal kitchens while being supplemented by many outside influences. Even though they are worlds apart in terms of wealth, the underlying ingredients and recipes used, as well as the styles of cooking, were, and still are, not much different between court and country. Presentation, with intricate artistry employed, and, to a certain extent, the superior quality of the ingredients available to the court, were what elevated the cuisine of the royal kitchens above that of the common people. The palaces put much effort into the teaching of culinary skills and crafts in order to maintain their proud reputations.

Geographically, culinary ideas have seeped into Thailand through the borders with Malaysia, Laos, Cambodia and Burma. China, who had a far-reaching influence on the entire region, has also made her mark on Thai cuisine. As would be expected, influences are strongest nearest the borders. The dishes found along the Mekong River have close affiliations to Laos, Cambodia and Vietnam. Around Chiang Mai there are Burmese-style curries and soups, and close to Malaysia, Muslim recipes such as massaman are common.

The most significant addition to Thai cuisine came not from Asia but from South America, via Europe. In the sixteenth century the Portuguese introduced what is now one of the hallmarks of the cuisine, the chilli. Thai cuisine, like that of other cultures that accepted the chilli so readily, had long included an element of heat by way of fresh green peppercorns, dried white peppercorns and galangal. As well, foreign vegetables and fruit have been cultivated for the last few centuries: tomatoes, eggplants (aubergines), asparagus, carrots (known as orange long turnips), corn and snow peas (mangetout) are common.

Thai food is, on the whole, made to be shared. Everything on the table is an accompaniment to rice, the most important component of the meal. Generally the rice is served with a curry, a fish dish, a stir-fry, a salad, a soup and vegetables. All the food is served at once. Soups come in a large bowl and are eaten with the meal, not before it. Meals begin when the host says 'kin khao' or 'eat rice'. The food is not necessarily eaten piping hot.

Thai people eat with a spoon and fork, the fork being used to push food onto the spoon or to pick up pieces of meat or sliced fruit. Chopsticks are

only used with noodles, and sticky rice and its accompaniments are eaten using the right hand. When eating in Thailand there are further subtle areas of etiquette to be observed. Platters of food are left on the table, and not passed around, as stretching is not considered rude and someone on the other side of the table will always be happy to spoon things onto your plate. You should take only a couple of spoonfuls of each dish at a time.

The north-east region of Thailand is known as Isaan and the food of the region is identified by the same name. Most of the area is a high plateau divided by the Phu Phan mountains. Divided from the rest of Thailand by more mountains, Laos and Cambodia, just over the border, have had a strong culinary influence, with much of the cuisines overlapping. The Mekong River flows along the border with both countries and has been the main means of trade for centuries.

North-eastern Thailand was one of the first areas in Asia to grow rice. Rice is cultivated over much of the plateau but rainfall is unreliable, making the yield patchy. Sticky rice is preferred in the countryside and long-grain rice in the cities. As much of the area is poorer than the rest of the country, food reflects this. Rice is a staple and dishes that are served with it are small in quantity but pungent in flavour. Unfermented fish sauce and chillies are the main seasonings. Pickled and preserved foods are a symptom of an unreliable food supply and also add more flavour to a diet of rice in this form than their fresh state.

Kai yang or kai ping (grilled chicken) is found all over the area. The chicken is rubbed with garlic, fish sauce, coriander (cilantro) root or lemon grass and black pepper, then flattened and pinned on a bamboo skewer before being barbecued over coals and served with a chilli dipping sauce. Chicken is also made into laap, a minced meat salad with lime juice, fish sauce, lemon grass, chillies or chilli powder and khao khua pon (roasted rice). Duck, fish and buffalo are also used to make laap, and grilled strips of beef are used for similar salads.

Som tam, a green papaya salad with chillies, peanuts, cherry tomatoes and dried shrimp, is a popular snack. Individual portions are pounded together by hand and eaten with sticky rice. Soups are hot and sour style (tom) or spicy style (sukii). The very south of the region has some coconut milk in soups.

Insects and frogs are popular, and red ants are used as a souring agent in some dishes. Fish are freshwater, the Mekong River being famous for the giant catfish caught from it, mainly in the months of April and May.

Northern Thailand, which is the area bordered by Burma to the west and Laos to the east, has always had a strong regional identity that is distinctively different from south and central Thailand. Hill tribes farm the hillsides, growing corn and rice, and families work as collectives, helping one another during planting and harvest time. The cooler climate of the hills means that many types of European fruit grow well, so peaches, apples and strawberries are found growing alongside lychees. Vegetables such as asparagus, snow peas (mangetout) and corn are also cultivated.

Above all the other dishes of the area, northern Thai curries have Burmese influences. Made without coconut milk, they are fiery and thinner in consistency. Kaeng hangleh muu, Chiang Mai pork curry, is the most famous. Naam phrik (chilli dips) are also popular, served with cooked or raw vegetables and crunchy deep-fried pork rind.

Pork is more popular in this region, eaten in its natural state and made into sausages. Fermented sausages made with pork rind and sticky rice are common, as are sausages made with pork and chillies. German-style frankfurters appear in salads, just one of the influences that American soldiers, stationed in the area during the Vietnam war, had on the cuisine.

Khao niaw (sticky rice) is the preferred rice, and can be bought ready-cooked wrapped in banana leaves, or in plastic bags, at markets. Noodles are popular due to the large amounts of Chinese and Burmese people who live in the area. Khao sawy, flat egg noodles with curry, is a speciality of Chiang Mai. Rice noodles are also popular and mung bean noodles are used in salads and soups as well as being wrapped in rice paper rolls.

Formal meals are served in small bowls on a teak platter. Another speciality of the area is insects. Deep-fried bamboo worm, water beetles and other insects are sold as snacks.

Central Thailand runs upwards from the Isthmus of Kra and encompasses the plains north of Bangkok. To the east it stretches to the Cambodian border, and to the west as far as Burma. Much of this area, watered by many rivers, constitutes the rice-bowl of Thailand. A network of canals further irrigates the region, as well as providing a means of transport. Paddy fields cover most of the area, but fruit, sugar cane, maize, peanuts and taro are also cultivated on a large scale.

The cuisine of Central Thailand is generally considered to be 'classic Thai' and includes the most recognizable Thai dishes.

Though most of this area has no access to the sea, the waterways provide a host of freshwater fish, prawns (shrimp) and crabs. Crabs and fish even live amongst the paddy as do the frogs and water beetles that are commonly eaten. Chicken, pork and beef also feature in the cuisine. The fertility of these regions means many vegetables grow easily, including Thai eggplants (aubergines), cha-om (a bitter green vegetable that resembles a fern) and bamboo shoots, as well as snake beans and European vegetables like tomatoes.

The cuisine of central Thailand is generally considered to be 'classic Thai' and includes the most recognizable Thai dishes. Curries include red, green and phanaeng (panaeng). Soups are tom khaa kai, tom yam and kaeng jeut (bland soup); yam (salads) are popular as are stir-fries. Dishes influenced by the Chinese include those baked in clay pots, noodle dishes as well as braised dishes flavoured with Chinese spices. Japanese-style sukii (similar to sukiyaki) is also available.

Seasonings give the typical hot, sour, salty and sweet combination, and palm sugar (jaggery) makes many recipes sweeter than their southern counterparts. Si Racha on the Gulf of Thailand is famous for its chilli sauce and it appears as a condiment on virtually every table.

The 14 provinces that make up the area between the Isthmus of Kra and the Malaysian border have always been culturally different from the rest of the country. Once under the influence of the Indonesian Sriwijaya empire along with areas of Malaysia, Malay-Indonesian culture and religion is still apparent.

Seafood and fish are the predominate feature of southern cuisine. With two long coastlines, fresh fish and seafood is eaten in abundance, and even more of it is preserved by drying. Locally made shrimp paste and fish sauce are used in quantity.

Southern Thailand is the land of the palm tree. Coconut and oil palms are farmed as well as growing wild, fringing the beaches. Further up the Isthmus, sugar palms are grown for their sweet sap. Phuket is home to pineapple plantations and rice is cultivated wherever it can be persuaded to grow.

Thai (Buddhist) curries and soups are tempered and enriched by the addition of coconut milk or cream. Spices include turmeric and pepper, and chillies are used with abandon. 'Yellow' curries are popular. Muslim dishes use ghee and oil rather than coconut and use a larger range of fragrant spices including cardamom, cumin and cloves. Kaeng matsaman, an Indian-style curry, is at its best in the South. Indo-Malay dishes such as satay are popular as are Indian-style roti. Chinese-style dishes include rice noodles, barbecued meats, deep-fried snacks, steamed buns, and dumplings.

Coffee shops sell kopi (filtered coffee), and this, served with khao yam (cooked dry rice, toasted coconut, makrut (kaffir) lime leaves, bean sprouts and lemon grass), makes a typical breakfast in the southern areas of Thailand.

Chapter 1

SNACKS AND STREET FOOD

Throughout Thailand, snacks of astonishing variety are sold from small carts equipped with charcoal barbecues, steamers, woks or hotplates. Each vendor of street food specializes in one type of cooking.

ข้าวผัด ล...

ผัดกระเ...

ผัดพ...

THUNG TONG

Gold Bags

This delicate Chinese-style starter or snack looks exactly as it is described – a tiny gold bag. Blanched chives will also work as ties for the tops of the bags. If you like you can use half prawns and half chicken or pork for the filling.

280 g (10 oz) raw prawns (shrimp), peeled, deveined and roughly chopped, or boneless, skinless chicken or pork fillet, roughly chopped

225 g (8 oz) tin water chestnuts, drained and roughly chopped

3–4 garlic cloves, finely chopped

3 spring onions (scallions), thinly sliced

1 tablespoon oyster sauce

1 teaspoon ground white pepper

1 teaspoon salt

2–3 bunches of spring onions (scallions), or 40 chives, for ties

2 tablespoons plain (all-purpose) flour

40 spring roll sheets, 13 cm (5 in) square

peanut oil, for deep-frying

a chilli sauce, to serve

Using a food processor or blender, chop the prawns, chicken or pork to a fine paste. Transfer to a bowl and combine with the water chestnuts, garlic, spring onions, oyster sauce, white pepper and salt.

To make spring onion ties, cut each into four to six strips, using only the longest green parts, then soak them in boiling water for 5 minutes, or until soft. Drain, then dry on paper towels.

Mix the flour and 160 ml (6 fl oz) cold water in a small saucepan until smooth. Stir and cook over medium heat for 1–2 minutes, or until thick.

Place three spring roll sheets in front of you and keep the remaining sheets in the plastic bag to prevent them drying out. Spoon 2 teaspoons of filling into the middle of each sheet. Brush around the filling with flour paste, then pull up into a bag and pinch together to enclose the filling. Place on

a tray that is lightly dusted with plain (all-purpose) flour. Repeat until you have used all the filling and sheets. Tie a piece of spring onion twice around each bag and tie in a knot. Use chives if you prefer.

Heat 7.5 cm (3 in) oil in a wok or deep frying pan over medium heat. When the oil seems hot, drop a small piece of spring roll sheet into it. If it sizzles immediately, the oil is ready. It is important not to have the oil too hot or the gold bags will cook too quickly and brown. Lower four bags into the oil and deep-fry for 2–3 minutes until they start to go hard. Lower another three or four bags into the oil and deep-fry them all together. To help cook the tops, splash the oil over the tops and deep-fry for 7–10 minutes, or until golden and crisp. As each batch is cooked, lift the bags out with a slotted spoon and add another batch. Drain on paper towels. Keep the gold bags warm while deep-frying the rest. Serve with a chilli sauce.

MAKES 40

KUNG HOM PAR

Prawns in a Blanket

These prawns, which are prepared in Chinese style, make a delicious canapé. Choose large plump prawns and leave the tails on for attractive presentation and ease of eating. Marinate the prawns overnight in the refrigerator if you want to prepare ahead.

12 raw large prawns (shrimp)
1 tablespoon plain (all-purpose) flour
2 garlic cloves, roughly chopped
3 coriander (cilantro) roots, finely chopped
1 cm (1/2 in) piece of ginger, roughly sliced
1 1/2 tablespoons oyster sauce or, for a hotter flavour,
   1/2 teaspoon red curry paste (page 236)

a sprinkle of ground white pepper
12 frozen spring roll sheets or filo sheets, 12 cm (5 in)
   square, defrosted
peanut oil, for deep-frying
a chilli sauce, or plum sauce (page 242), to serve

Peel and devein the prawns, leaving the tails intact. To make the prawns easier to wrap, you can make three or four shallow incisions in the underside of each, then open up the cuts to straighten out the prawns.

Mix the flour and 3 tablespoons water in a small saucepan until smooth. Stir and cook over medium heat for 1–2 minutes, or until thick.

Using a pestle and mortar or small blender, pound or blend the garlic, coriander and ginger together.

In a bowl, combine the garlic paste with the prawns, oyster sauce, pepper and a pinch of salt. Cover with plastic wrap and marinate in the refrigerator for 2 hours, turning occasionally.

Place a spring roll or filo sheet on the work surface and keep the remaining sheets in the plastic bag to prevent them drying out. Fold the sheet in half,

remove a prawn from the marinade and place it on the sheet with its tail sticking out of the top. Fold up the bottom and then fold in the sides to tightly enclose the prawn. Seal the joins with the flour paste. Repeat with the rest of the prawns and wrappers.

Heat the oil in a wok or deep frying pan over medium heat. When the oil seems hot, drop a small piece of spring roll sheet into it. If it sizzles immediately, the oil is ready. Deep-fry four prawns at a time for 3–4 minutes, or until golden brown and crisp. Remove with a slotted spoon and drain on paper towels. Keep the prawns warm while deep-frying the rest.

Transfer to a serving plate. Serve hot with chilli sauce or plum sauce.

SERVES 4

MIANG KHAM

Betel Leaves with Savoury Topping

2 tablespoons peanut oil
4 Asian shallots, thinly sliced
2 garlic cloves, smashed with the side of a cleaver
150 g (6 oz) minced (ground) chicken or pork
2 tablespoons fish sauce
1 tablespoon tamarind purée
1 tablespoon dried shrimp, chopped

2 tablespoons palm sugar (jaggery)
1 cm (1/2 in) piece of ginger, grated
2 bird's eye chillies, finely chopped
1 tablespoon roasted peanuts, chopped
1 tablespoon chopped coriander (cilantro) leaves
16 betel leaves
lime wedges, for squeezing

Heat the peanut oil in a wok and fry the shallots and garlic for 1–2 minutes, or until brown. Add the chicken and fry until the meat turns opaque, breaking up any lumps. Add the fish sauce, tamarind purée, shrimp and palm sugar and cook until the mixture is brown and sticky. Stir in the ginger, chillies, peanuts and coriander leaves.

Arrange the betel leaves on a platter and top each with some of the mixture. Serve with lime wedges.

MAKES 16

MAR HOR

Galloping Horses

1 1/2 tablespoons vegetable oil
2–3 garlic cloves, finely chopped
225 g (8 oz) minced (ground) pork
1 spring onion (scallion), thinly sliced
1/2 tablespoon coriander (cilantro) leaves, finely chopped
25 g (1 oz) unsalted cooked peanuts, roughly ground

2 tablespoons light soy sauce
3 tablespoons palm sugar (jaggery)
a pinch of ground white pepper
16 small segments of pineapple
a few coriander (cilantro) leaves, for garnish
1 red chilli, very thinly sliced, for garnish

Heat the oil in a saucepan or wok and stir-fry the garlic until golden brown. Add the pork and cook over medium heat, using a spoon to break up the meat until it has separated and is almost dry. Add the spring onion, coriander, peanuts, soy sauce, sugar and pepper. Stir together for 4–5 minutes, or until the mixture is dry and sticky.

Arrange the pineapple on a platter and top each segment with a little of the pork mixture. Place a coriander leaf and a slice of chilli on top of each.

SERVES 4

Paw Pia Thawt

Spring Rolls

These savoury rolls are popular throughout Southeast Asia. The Thai version is a delicate cross between Chinese and Vietnamese styles. Thai spring rolls are deep-fried until light golden brown and crisp. They can be served with chilli or light soy sauce.

50 g (2 oz) vermicelli, cellophane or wun sen noodles
15 g (1/2 oz) dried black fungus (about half a handful)
2 tablespoons plain (all-purpose) flour
1 1/2 tablespoons vegetable oil
3–4 garlic cloves, finely chopped
100 g (4 oz) minced (ground) chicken or pork
1 small carrot, finely grated
140 g (5 oz/1 2/3 cups) bean sprouts

1 cm (1/2 in) piece of ginger, finely grated
1 1/2–2 tablespoons fish sauce
1 1/2 tablespoons oyster sauce
1/4 teaspoon ground white pepper
25 spring roll sheets, 13 cm (5 in) square
peanut oil, for deep-frying
a chilli sauce, to serve

Soak the vermicelli in hot water for 1–2 minutes, or until soft. Drain, then cut into small pieces. Soak the dried mushrooms in hot water for 2–3 minutes, or until soft. Drain, then finely chop. To make a paste, stir the flour and 2 tablespoons of water together in a small bowl until smooth.

Heat the oil in a wok or frying pan and stir-fry the garlic until golden brown. Add the chicken or pork and, using a spoon, break up the meat until it has separated and is cooked through. Add the vermicelli, mushrooms, carrot, bean sprouts, ginger, fish sauce, oyster sauce and white pepper. Cook for another 4–5 minutes, then adjust the seasoning. Allow to cool.

Place 3 spring roll sheets on a work surface and spread some flour paste around the edges. Keep the remaining sheets in the plastic bag. Spoon 2 teaspoons of filling onto a sheet along the side nearest to you, about 2.5 cm (1 in) from the edge.

Bring the edge up, then roll it away from you a half turn over the filling. Fold the sides into the centre to enclose the filling, then wrap and seal the join with the flour paste. Repeat with the rest of the filling and wrappers. (At this stage, the spring rolls can be frozen. If freezing, wrap each roll with another spring roll sheet.)

Heat 5 cm (2 in) oil in a wok or deep frying pan over medium heat. When the oil seems hot, drop a small piece of spring roll sheet into the oil. If it sizzles immediately, the oil is ready. Don't have the oil too hot. Lower five rolls into the oil and deep-fry for 2–3 minutes. When they start to go hard, lower another four rolls into the oil and deep-fry them all together. To help cook the tops, splash oil over the tops. Deep-fry for 6–8 minutes, or until crisp. As the spring rolls cook, lift out one at a time with a slotted spoon and add another. Drain on paper towels. Serve with a chilli sauce.

PICTURE ON PAGE 22

MAKES 25 SMALL SPRING ROLLS

Spring Rolls
(recipe on page 21)

Khai Luk Koei

Son-in-law Eggs

A traditional celebration dish, these eggs are enjoyed on New Year's Day or at wedding feasts, and are taken as an offering to the monks when Thai people visit their local temple. They make good snacks. Deep-frying gives the skins a unique texture.

2 dried long red chillies, about 13 cm (5 in) long
vegetable oil, for deep-frying
110 g (4 oz) Asian shallots, thinly sliced
6 large hard-boiled eggs, shelled

2 tablespoons fish sauce
3 tablespoons tamarind purée
5 tablespoons palm sugar (jaggery)

Cut the dried chillies into 5 mm (¼ in) pieces with scissors or a knife and discard the seeds. Heat 5 cm (2 in) oil in a wok or deep frying pan over medium heat. When the oil seems hot, drop a slice of the Asian shallot into the oil. If it sizzles straight away, the oil is ready. Deep-fry the chillies for a few seconds, being careful not to burn them, to bring out the flavour. Remove them with a slotted spoon, then drain on paper towels.

In the same wok, deep-fry the Asian shallots for 3–4 minutes until golden brown. Be careful not to burn them. Remove with a slotted spoon, then drain on paper towels.

Use a spoon to slide one egg at a time into the same hot oil. Be careful as the oil may splash. Deep-fry for 10–15 minutes, or until each egg is golden brown all over. Remove with a slotted spoon, then drain on paper towels. Keep warm.

In a saucepan over medium heat, stir the fish sauce, tamarind purée and sugar for 5–7 minutes, or until all the sugar has dissolved.

Halve the eggs lengthways and arrange them with the yolk upwards on a serving plate. Drizzle the tamarind sauce over the eggs and sprinkle the crisp chillies and shallots over them.

SERVES 4

When the eggs are golden, they are ready. Carefully remove with a slotted spoon and drain on paper towels.

Sa-te Kai

Chicken Satay

Originating in Indonesia, satay has made its way north and has been adapted to suit local taste. Satay should be cooked quickly over hot charcoals. Traditionally served with peanut sauce, it is also delicious with cucumber relish or sweet chilli sauce.

1 kg (2 lb 4 oz) boneless, skinless chicken breast

MARINADE
2–3 Asian shallots, roughly chopped
4–5 garlic cloves, roughly chopped
4 coriander (cilantro) roots, finely chopped
2.5 cm (1 in) piece of ginger, sliced
1 tablespoon roasted ground coriander
1 tablespoon roasted ground cumin
1 tablespoon roasted ground turmeric
1 teaspoon curry powder (page 243) or bought Thai curry powder
2 tablespoons light soy sauce
4 tablespoons vegetable oil
410 ml (14 fl oz/$1^2/_3$ cups) coconut milk (page 245)
2 tablespoons palm sugar (jaggery)
$1^1/_2$ teaspoons salt
peanut sauce (page 242) or cucumber relish (page 243), to serve

Cut the chicken into strips 4 cm ($1^1/_2$ in) wide x 10 cm (4 in) long x 5 mm ($1/_4$ in) thick and put them in a bowl.

Using a food processor, blender or pestle and mortar, blend or pound the shallots, garlic, coriander roots and ginger to a paste.

Add the paste to the chicken, along with the ground coriander, cumin, turmeric, curry powder, light soy sauce, vegetable oil, coconut milk, sugar and salt. Mix with your fingers or a spoon until the chicken is well coated. Cover with plastic wrap and marinate in the refrigerator for at least 5 hours, or overnight. Turn the chicken occasionally.

Soak 40 bamboo sticks, about 18–20 cm (7–8 in) long, in water for 1 hour to prevent them from burning during cooking.

Thread a piece of the marinated chicken onto each bamboo stick. If the pieces are small, thread two pieces onto each stick.

Heat a barbecue or grill (broiler) to high. If using the grill, line the tray with foil.

Barbecue the satay sticks for 5–7 minutes on each side, or grill (broil) for 10 minutes on each side, until the chicken is cooked through and slightly charred. Turn frequently and brush the marinade sauce over the meat during cooking. If using the grill, cook a good distance below the heat. Serve hot with peanut sauce or cucumber relish.

MAKES 40 STICKS

Khao Phoht Thawt
Sweet Corn Cakes

400 g (14 oz/2 cups) corn kernels
1 egg
3 tablespoons rice flour
1 tablespoon yellow curry paste (page 238)
2 tablespoons chopped Asian shallots

1 tablespoon fish sauce
25 g (1 oz/½ cup) roughly chopped coriander (cilantro)
1 large red chilli, chopped
peanut oil, for shallow-frying
cucumber relish (page 243), to serve

Combine the corn kernels, egg, rice flour, curry paste, shallots, fish sauce, coriander and chilli in a bowl. Shape the mixture into small patties, adding more rice flour, if necessary, to combine into a soft mixture.

Heat the oil in a wok or frying pan and fry the corn cakes for 3–4 minutes, turning once, until golden brown. Serve hot with cucumber relish.

MAKES 8

Khanom Bang Na Kung
Sesame Prawns on Toasts

280 g (10 oz) raw prawns (shrimp), peeled and deveined
2 teaspoons light soy sauce
1 egg
7–8 coriander (cilantro) roots, roughly chopped
4–5 large garlic cloves, roughly chopped
¼ teaspoon ground white pepper

½ teaspoon salt
7 slices day-old white bread, crusts removed, each slice cut into two triangles
3 tablespoons sesame seeds
peanut oil, for deep-frying
cucumber relish (page 243), to serve

Using a food processor or blender, chop the prawns into a smooth paste. Transfer to a bowl, add the light soy sauce and egg and mix well. Leave for about 30 minutes to firm.

Using a pestle and mortar, pound the coriander roots, garlic, pepper and salt into a smooth paste. Add to the prawns. (Using a pestle and mortar gives the best texture but you can also process the coriander roots, garlic, pepper, salt, light soy sauce and egg with the prawns.) Heat the grill (broiler) to medium. Spread the bread on a baking tray and grill for 3–4 minutes, or until the bread is dry and slightly crisp. Spread the prawn paste thickly on one side of each piece. Sprinkle with sesame seeds and press on firmly. Refrigerate for 30 minutes.

Heat the oil in a wok or deep frying pan over medium heat. Drop in a small cube of bread. If it sizzles immediately, the oil is ready. Deep-fry a few toasts at a time, paste-side down, for 3 minutes, or until golden. Turn with a slotted spoon. Drain on paper towels. Serve hot with cucumber relish.

MAKES 14

KARII PUFF
Curry Puffs

FILLING

1½ tablespoons vegetable oil
2–3 garlic cloves, finely chopped
1 small onion, finely chopped
5 coriander (cilantro) roots, finely chopped
200 g (7 oz) minced (ground) chicken, pork or raw
    prawns (shrimp)
1 small red capsicum (pepper), finely diced
50 g (2 oz/⅓ cup) peas
350 g (12 oz) potatoes, peeled, cooked and cut
    into small dice
3 tablespoons fish sauce
2 tablespoons sugar

1 teaspoon curry powder (page 243) or bought
    Thai curry powder
peanut oil, for deep-frying

PASTRY A

340 g (12 oz/2¾ cups) self-raising flour
2 teaspoons sugar
½ teaspoon salt
80 ml (3 fl oz/⅓ cup) vegetable oil

PASTRY B

185 g (7 oz/1½ cups) self-raising flour
80–125 ml (3–4 fl oz/⅓–½ cup) vegetable oil

Heat the oil in a wok or frying pan and stir-fry the garlic. Add the onion and coriander roots and cook over medium heat for 2–3 minutes. Stir in the chicken, breaking it up until it is separated and cooked. Add the capsicum and peas and stir for 1–2 minutes. Stir in the potatoes, fish sauce, sugar and curry powder. Adjust the seasoning.

To make pastry A, combine the flour, sugar and salt in a bowl. Make a well and pour in the oil. Gradually add 125–170 ml (4–6 fl oz/½–⅔ cup) water and gently knead until the dough is smooth. Make 15 balls, place them on a tray and cover with plastic wrap. To make pastry B, lightly mix the flour and oil until the dough just holds together. Make 15 balls, place on a tray and cover.

Roll a ball of pastry A into a disc, wrap it around a ball of pastry B, then squeeze them together. Roll out a 5 x 15 cm (2 x 6 in) rectangle. Take the short edge of the rectangle and roll up tightly into a tube. Using a rolling pin, flatten the pastry lengthways to form a rectangle. Repeat one more time, rolling and flattening the pastry. Roll into a tube and cut

in half. You should see the different layers of pastry in the cross section. To use, take one half, turn it vertically so that it rests on the cut section and roll it into a round sheet. Place the sheet on the work surface and spoon 1–1½ tablespoons of filling onto the middle. Brush the pastry edge with water and fold over to form a semicircle. Press the edges to seal. Make repeated folds on the rounded edge by folding a little piece of the pastry over as you move around the edge. Place on a tray and repeat with the remaining pastry and filling.

Heat 7.5 cm (3 in) oil in a wok or deep frying pan over medium heat. Drop a small piece of pastry into the oil. If it sizzles immediately, the oil is ready. Don't have the oil too hot. Lower in three or four of the puffs. After 2 minutes they will rise. Lower in another two to three and deep-fry them all together. To help cook the tops, splash oil over the tops. Deep-fry for 3–4 minutes, or until they puff up. As each batch cooks, lift out with a slotted spoon and add more puffs to the oil. Drain on paper towels. Serve hot, warm or cold.

MAKES 30

STREET FOOD

Thais like to eat at all hours of the day. Street or hawker food is a subculture that thrives all over the country. Rot khen (vendor carts) are parked by the roadside in even the smallest village. Mostly found near markets during the day, hawker food comes into its own at dusk and into the night.

Virtually every dish in Thai cuisine can be bought from one type of stall or another, the exception being royal cuisine. Everything from meals with a choice of two or three dishes and rice, to simple snacks like satay, mussel pancakes and grilled bananas can be bought at any time of the day or night. Dishes like curries are pre-cooked but everything else is freshly made.

The hawker stalls are allowed to set up almost anywhere they like. They can be found around the edge of markets, beside busy roads, down back streets or close to bus stops and stations. Stalls can be simple carts, which are pushed home every night, or they can be more permanent. Those that have a good reputation last for years, decades, and even generations on the same spot.

There are five basic types of street food identifiable by the type of stall that sells them. Look out for the right type of cart and it will have the dish you are looking for. Carts with glass showcases sell dishes like som tam (green papaya salad), noodle dishes and soups, roast pork and chicken and Chinese chicken rice. Stalls with charcoal barbecues sell satay, barbecued chicken and pork, Thai sausages, dried squid and grilled bananas. Steamer domes indicate red braised pork, Chinese dumplings and buns, pumpkin custard and sticky rice in banana leaves. Carts fitted with a large hotplate make mussels in batter, omelettes, pancakes and fried noodles. Woks mean spring rolls, won tons, fish cakes and dough sticks.

Ready-cooked food comes from vendors with prepared dishes such as fish curry in banana cups, pork-rind soups and lots of different puddings such as sticky rice. Drinks carts sell fruit juices and sweets served over crushed ice. Other specialist carts sell fresh fruit, preserved fruit and seafood, including boiled clams or cockles. Pieces of roast pork are popular, sold with two types of dipping sauce. Corn on the cob is a relatively new introduction. Chinese-style soups are a favourite at lunchtime and insects of various types, such as deep-fried cockroaches with a chilli dipping sauce, are common in the northern part of Thailand.

THAWT MAN PLAA

Fried Fish Cakes with Green Beans

Fish cakes are just one of many delicious snacks sold as street food in Thailand. Batches are fried on request and served in a plastic bag, along with a bamboo skewer for eating them and a small bag of sauce for additional flavour.

450 g (1 lb) firm white fish fillets
1 tablespoon red curry paste (page 236) or bought paste
1 tablespoon fish sauce
1 egg
50 g (2 oz) snake (yard-long) beans, thinly sliced

5 makrut (kaffir) lime leaves, finely shredded
peanut oil, for deep-frying
sweet chilli sauce (page 241), to serve
cucumber relish (page 243), to serve

Remove any skin and bone from the fish and roughly chop the flesh. In a food processor or a blender, mince the fish fillets until smooth. Add the curry paste, fish sauce and egg, then blend briefly until smooth. Spoon into a bowl and mix in the beans and makrut lime leaves. Use wet hands to shape the fish paste into thin, flat cakes, about 5 cm (2 in) across, using about a tablespoon of mixture for each.

Heat 5 cm (2 in) oil in a wok or deep frying pan over medium heat. When the oil seems hot, drop a small piece of fish cake into it. If it sizzles immediately, the oil is ready.

Lower five or six of the fish cakes into the oil and deep-fry them until they are golden brown on both sides and very puffy. Remove with a slotted spoon and drain on paper towels. Keep the cooked fish cakes warm while deep-frying the rest. Serve hot with sweet chilli sauce and cucumber relish.

For a variation, make up another batch of the fish mixture but leave out the curry paste. Cook as above and serve both types together.

MAKES 30

Using wet hands makes the fish mixture less likely to stick to your hands and also easier to handle.

Khao Niaw Na Kung
Sticky Rice with Shrimp or Coconut Topping

SHRIMP TOPPING

2 garlic cloves, roughly chopped

4 coriander (cilantro) roots, cleaned

¼ teaspoon ground black pepper

1 tablespoon vegetable oil

200 g (7 oz) minced (ground) shrimp or very small
  raw prawns (shrimp)

25 g (1 oz) grated coconut (page 247)

1 teaspoon fish sauce

3 tablespoons sugar

COCONUT TOPPING

150 g (6 oz) grated coconut or desiccated coconut

150 g (6 oz) palm sugar (jaggery)

1 quantity of steamed sticky rice with coconut milk
  (page 247)

3 makrut (kaffir) lime leaves, thinly sliced, for garnish

To make the shrimp topping, use a pestle and mortar to pound the garlic, coriander roots and pepper to a smooth paste. Alternatively, chop with a sharp knife until smooth. Heat the oil in a wok or frying pan and stir-fry the garlic mixture over medium heat until fragrant. Add the minced shrimp or prawns, coconut, fish sauce and sugar and stir-fry for 3–4 minutes, or until the minced shrimp is cooked. Taste, then adjust the seasoning if necessary. The flavour should be sweet and lightly salty.

To make the coconut topping, mix the coconut, sugar, 125 ml (4 fl oz/½ cup) water and a pinch of salt in a saucepan and stir over low heat until the sugar has dissolved. Do not let it thicken to a point where it will harden. Remove from the heat.

Serve by filling a small, wet bowl with the sticky rice and turning it out on a small plate. Top with shrimp or coconut topping and a sprinkle of lime leaves. You can use half of each topping if you like.

SERVES 4

HAWY THAWT
Fried Mussel Pancake

2 kg (4 lb 8 oz) small black mussels in their shells
  (yielding around 350 g/12 oz meat)

CHILLI SAUCE
1 long red chilli, seeded and finely chopped
2 1/2 tablespoons white vinegar
1/2 teaspoon sugar

50 g (2 oz) tapioca or plain (all-purpose) flour
40 g (1 1/2 oz/1/3 cup) cornflour (cornstarch)
1 tablespoon fish sauce

1 teaspoon sugar
6 garlic cloves, finely chopped
350 g (12 oz/4 cups) bean sprouts
4 spring onions (scallions), sliced
80 ml (3 fl oz/1/3 cup) vegetable oil
4 large eggs
a few coriander (cilantro) leaves
1 long red chilli, seeded and thinly sliced
a sprinkle of ground white pepper
4 lime wedges

Preheat the oven to 180°C (350°F/Gas 4). Scrub the mussels and remove their hairy beards. Discard any open mussels and any that don't close when tapped on the work surface. Spread the mussels over a baking tray and bake for 5 minutes, or until the shells open slightly. Discard any unopened mussels. When the shells return to a comfortable temperature, prise them open, scoop out the meat from each and put it in a colander to drain out any juices.

To make the chilli sauce, mix the chilli, vinegar, sugar and a pinch of salt in a small serving bowl.

Combine the flours with 6 to 8 tablespoons water using a fork or spoon until the mixture is smooth and without lumps. Add the fish sauce and sugar. Divide among four bowls and add some mussels to each bowl.

Separate the garlic, bean sprouts and spring onions into equal portions for each serving.

Make one pancake at a time. Heat 1 tablespoon oil in a small frying pan and stir-fry one portion of garlic over medium heat until golden brown. Stir one portion of the mussel mixture with a spoon and pour it into the frying pan, swirling the pan to ensure that the mixture spreads evenly. Cook for 2–3 minutes, or until it is brown underneath. Turn with a spatula and brown the other side. Make a hole in the centre and break an egg into the hole. Sprinkle a half portion of bean sprouts and spring onion over the top. Cook until the egg sets, then flip the pancake again. Turn the pancake onto a serving plate.

Sprinkle each pancake with coriander leaves, sliced chilli and ground pepper. Place a lime wedge, bean sprouts and spring onions on the plate. Serve with the chilli sauce.

SERVES 4

SOM TAM MALAKAW

Green Papaya Salad

This dish from the north-east is now popular throughout Thailand. Som means 'sour', and Tam means 'pounded' (with a pestle and mortar). Multiply the ingredients by the number of portions but make just one serve at a time so it will fit in your mortar.

120 g (4 oz) small hard, green, unripe papaya
1½ tablespoons palm sugar (jaggery)
1 tablespoon fish sauce
1–2 garlic cloves
25 g (1 oz) roasted peanuts
25 g (1 oz) snake (yard-long) beans, cut into 2.5 cm (1 in) pieces

1 tablespoon ground dried shrimp
2–6 bird's eye chillies, stems removed (6 will give a very hot result)
50 g (2 oz) cherry tomatoes, left whole, or 2 medium tomatoes, cut into 6 wedges
half a lime
sticky rice (page 246), to serve

Peel the green papaya with a vegetable peeler and cut the papaya into long, thin shreds. If you have a mandolin, use the grater attachment.

Mix the palm sugar with the fish sauce until the sugar has dissolved.

Using a large, deep pestle and mortar, pound the garlic into a paste. Add the roasted peanuts and pound roughly with the garlic. Add the papaya and pound softly, using a spoon to scrape down the side, and turning and mixing well.

Add the beans, dried shrimp and chillies and keep pounding and turning to bruise these ingredients.

Add the palm sugar mixture and the tomatoes, squeeze in the lime juice and add the lime skin to the mixture. Lightly pound together for another minute until thoroughly mixed. As the juice comes out, pound more gently so that the liquid doesn't splash. Discard the lime skin. Taste the sauce in the bottom of the mortar and adjust the seasoning if necessary. It should be a balance of sweet and sour with a hot and salty taste.

Spoon the papaya salad and all the juices onto a serving plate. Serve with sticky rice.

SERVES 1

Far left: Pound the papaya with the garlic and peanut mixture.

Left: Use a spoon to scrape down the side of the mortar as you turn and mix the salad.

Kung Phat Bai Phak Chii Lae Phrik
Prawns with Coriander Leaves and Chilli

350 g (12 oz) raw prawns (shrimp)
1 garlic clove, finely chopped
1 tablespoon coriander (cilantro) leaves, finely chopped
½–1 long red chilli, seeded and finely chopped
2 teaspoons lime juice
2 teaspoons vegetable oil

1 teaspoon sesame oil
1½ teaspoons light soy sauce
1 tablespoon oyster sauce
¼ teaspoon ground white pepper
4 bamboo sticks

Peel and devein the prawns and cut each prawn along the back so it opens like a butterfly (leave each prawn joined along the base and at the tail).

Put the garlic, coriander, chilli, lime juice, both oils, light soy sauce, oyster sauce and pepper in a shallow dish and mix well. Add the prawns and mix to coat. Cover with plastic wrap and refrigerate for at least 30 minutes, or overnight.

Soak the bamboo sticks in water for 1 hour to help prevent them from burning during cooking.

Heat a barbecue or grill (broiler) to a high heat. If you are using a grill, line the tray with foil.

Thread the marinated prawns onto the skewers and grill (broil) a good distance below the heat for 8–10 minutes on each side. If you cook them directly on a barbecue plate they will cook in about 4–5 minutes. Turn the prawns frequently until they turn pink and are cooked through. You can brush the marinade sauce over the prawns during cooking. Serve hot.

SERVES 4

Sai Ua
Pork Sausages

3 coriander (cilantro) roots
1 lemon grass stalk, white part only, chopped
4 garlic cloves, chopped
½ teaspoon ground white pepper

1 small red chilli, chopped
2 teaspoons fish sauce
2 teaspoons sugar
300 g (11 oz) minced (ground) pork

Using a pestle and mortar or food processor, pound or blend the coriander, lemon grass, garlic and pepper to a fine paste. Add the chilli, fish sauce, sugar and pork to the paste mixture and combine well. Form into sausage shapes.

Heat a barbecue or grill (broiler) to a high heat and cook the sausages for 4–5 minutes each side, or until cooked through.

SERVES 4

KAI HAW BAI TOEY

Chicken Wrapped in Pandanus Leaf

Pandanus leaves act as both a wrapping and a flavouring in this dish. Leaving a long tail on the parcels will make them prettier and easier to handle so don't trim the leaves. To eat, carefully unwrap the parcels and dip the chicken in the sauce.

5 coriander (cilantro) roots, cleaned and roughly chopped
4–5 garlic cloves
1 teaspoon ground white pepper
¼ teaspoon salt
600 g (1 lb 5 oz) boneless, skinless chicken breast,
 cut into 25 cubes

2 tablespoons oyster sauce
1½ tablespoons sesame oil
1 tablespoon plain (all-purpose) flour
25 pandanus leaves, cleaned and dried
vegetable oil, for deep-frying
plum sauce (page 242) or a chilli sauce, to serve

Using a pestle and mortar or a small blender, pound or blend the coriander roots, garlic, white pepper and salt into a paste.

In a bowl, combine the paste with the chicken, oyster sauce, sesame oil and flour. Cover with plastic wrap and marinate in the refrigerator for at least 3 hours, or overnight.

Fold one of the pandanus leaves, bringing the base up in front of the tip, making a cup. Put a piece of chicken in the fold and, moving the bottom of the leaf, wrap it around to create a tie and enclose the chicken. Repeat until you have used all the chicken.

Heat the oil in a wok or deep frying pan over medium heat. When the oil seems hot, drop a small piece of pandanus leaf into it. If it sizzles immediately, the oil is ready. Lower some parcels into the oil and deep-fry them for 7–10 minutes, or until the parcels feel firm. Lift out with a slotted spoon and drain on paper towels. Keep the cooked parcels warm while deep-frying the rest. Transfer to a serving plate and serve with plum sauce or a chilli sauce.

MAKES 25

Right: Fold the pandanus leaf to make a cup, and put a piece of chicken inside it.

Far right: Wrap the leaf around the chicken to enclose it.

Chapter 2

SOUPS

Aromatic soups (tom) are served with the other dishes in a meal and are not a course in themselves. They're ladled into small bowls and dipped into occasionally to counterbalance other flavours in the meal.

TOM YAM TAO-HUU

Fragrant Tofu and Tomato Soup

Tofu, or bean curd, comes in several different varieties, from soft to quite firm. The softest, called silken tofu, has the best type of texture for this recipe. The strong flavourings used in the recipe are a perfect contrast for the tofu.

PASTE
½ teaspoon dried shrimp paste
1 teaspoon small dried prawns (shrimp)
4 Asian shallots, roughly chopped
½ teaspoon white peppercorns
2 coriander (cilantro) roots
1 garlic clove, chopped
2 teaspoons grated ginger

1 tablespoon vegetable oil
750 ml (27 fl oz/3 cups) chicken stock or water

3 tablespoons tamarind purée
1 tablespoon palm sugar (jaggery)
2 tablespoons fish sauce
3 cm (1¼ in) piece of ginger, julienned
3 Asian shallots, smashed with the flat side of a cleaver
300 g (11 oz) silken tofu (bean curd), cut into 2 cm
  (¾ in) cubes
2 tomatoes, each cut into 8 wedges
1 tablespoon lime juice
2 tablespoons coriander (cilantro) leaves, for garnish

To make the paste, use a pestle and mortar or a food processor to pound or blend the shrimp paste, dried prawns, Asian shallots, white peppercorns, coriander roots, garlic and ginger together.

Heat the oil in a saucepan over low heat, add the paste and cook for 10–15 seconds, stirring constantly. Add the stock or water, tamarind purée, palm sugar, fish sauce and ginger. Simmer for 5 minutes to soften the ginger.

Add the shallots, tofu, tomatoes and lime juice to the pan and cook for 2–3 minutes to heat through. Garnish with coriander leaves.

SERVES 4

Tom Yam Kung

Hot and Sour Prawn Soup

This soup is probably the most well-known Thai dish of all. Although it is usually made with prawns, it works equally well with fish. To achieve the famous distinctive aroma and flavours, use only the freshest good-quality ingredients.

350 g (12 oz) raw prawns (shrimp)
1 tablespoon oil
3 lemon grass stalks, white part only, bruised
3 thin slices of galangal
2 litres (70 fl oz/8 cups) chicken stock or water
5–7 bird's eye chillies, stems removed, bruised
5 makrut (kaffir) lime leaves, torn

2 tablespoons fish sauce
70 g (2 oz) straw mushrooms, or quartered button
  mushrooms
2 spring onions (scallions), sliced
3 tablespoons lime juice
a few coriander (cilantro) leaves, for garnish

Peel and devein the prawns, leaving the tails intact and reserving the heads and shells. Heat the oil in a large stockpot or wok and add the prawn heads and shells. Cook for 5 minutes, or until the shells turn bright orange.

Add one stalk of lemon grass to the pan with the galangal and stock or water. Bring to the boil, then reduce the heat and simmer for 20 minutes. Strain the stock and return to the pan. Discard the shells and flavourings.

Thinly slice the remaining lemon grass and add it to the liquid with the chillies, lime leaves, fish sauce, mushrooms and spring onions. Cook gently for 2 minutes.

Add the prawns and cook for 3 minutes, or until the prawns are firm and pink. Take off the heat and add the lime juice. Taste, then adjust the seasoning with extra lime juice or fish sauce if necessary. Garnish with coriander leaves.

SERVES 4

Kaeng Jeut Phrak Kai

Vegetable Soup with Chicken and Prawns

A bland soup that is best served with a meal, to be eaten alongside the other main dishes. Bland soups help take the heat out of chilli dishes. The chicken balls in this soup are easily made but you could use cubes of chicken instead.

175 g (6 oz) raw prawns (shrimp)

2 coriander (cilantro) roots, cleaned and finely chopped

2 garlic cloves, roughly chopped

pinch of ground white pepper, plus extra, to sprinkle

150 g (6 oz) minced (ground) chicken

½ spring onion (scallion), finely chopped

935 ml (33 fl oz/3¾ cups) chicken or vegetable stock

2 tablespoons light soy sauce

2 teaspoons preserved radish

175 g (6 oz) marrow or pumpkin (squash), cut into 2.5 cm (1 in) cubes

175 g (6 oz) Chinese cabbage, roughly chopped

a few coriander (cilantro) leaves, for garnish

Peel and devein the prawns and cut each prawn along the back so it opens like a butterfly (leave each prawn joined along the base and at the tail, leaving the tail attached).

Using a pestle and mortar or a small blender, pound or blend the coriander roots, garlic, pepper and a pinch of salt into a paste. In a bowl, combine the coriander paste with the chicken and spring onion. Use a spoon or your wet hands to shape the chicken mixture into small balls about 1 cm (½ in) in diameter.

Pour the stock into a saucepan and bring to the boil. Add the light soy sauce and preserved radish. Lower the chicken balls into the stock and cook over medium heat for 1–2 minutes, or until the balls are cooked through.

Add the marrow or pumpkin to the pan and cook for 2–3 minutes. Add the prawns and Chinese cabbage and cook for another 1–2 minutes. Taste, then adjust the seasoning if necessary. Garnish with coriander leaves and sprinkle with ground white pepper.

SERVES 4

Far left: Make a paste using the coriander roots, garlic, white pepper and salt.

Left: Combine the coriander paste with the chicken and spring onion and shape the mixture into small balls.

Kaeng Jeut Tao-Huu Sai Kung
Stuffed Tofu Soup with Prawns

This recipe is quite fiddly but well worth the effort. Don't overstuff the tofu or it might explode out as it cooks. As with other 'bland' soups, use a good-quality stock. The stuffed tofu can also be fried and eaten on its own.

275 g (10 oz) raw prawns (shrimp)
2–3 coriander (cilantro) roots, roughly chopped
2 garlic cloves, roughly chopped
¼ teaspoon salt
1 tablespoon cornflour (cornstarch)
¼ teaspoon ground white pepper

320 g (11 oz) firm tofu (bean curd)
1.5 litres (52 fl oz/6 cups) vegetable stock
2.5 cm (1 in) piece of ginger, sliced
80 ml (3 fl oz/⅓ cup) light soy sauce
1 tablespoon preserved radish
5 spring onions (scallions), cut into slivers, for garnish

Peel and devein the prawns. Set aside about 80 g (3 oz) of the prawns and cut the rest of them along their backs so they open like a butterfly (leave each prawn joined along the base and at the tail).

Using a food processor or a blender, chop the coriander roots and the garlic until as smooth as possible. Add the prawns that are not butterflied, along with the salt, cornflour and white pepper, then blend until as smooth as possible. If you prefer, you can use a pestle and mortar to pound the coriander roots and garlic into a paste before processing with the prawns. This gives a slightly better flavour.

Drain the tofu and cut it into 16 triangles. Cut a pocket into the long side of each piece of tofu with a knife. Spoon some prawn mixture into each pocket and gently press down on top. Repeat until you have used all the tofu and the mixture.

Heat the stock to boiling point in a saucepan. Reduce the heat to low and add the ginger, light soy sauce and preserved radish. Lower the tofu into the stock and cook for 4–5 minutes, or until cooked. Add the butterflied prawns and cook for another 1–2 minutes, or until the prawns open and turn pink. Taste, then adjust the seasoning if necessary. Serve garnished with spring onions.

SERVES 4

Far left: Carefully spoon the prawn filling into the pockets in the tofu triangles.

Left: Lower the tofu triangles into the boiling stock.

KAENG SOM PLA KUP PHAK BUNG
Sour Fish Soup with Water Spinach

SOUR CURRY PASTE
3 garlic cloves, roughly chopped
3 bird's eye chillies, stems removed
1 Asian shallot, chopped
1 teaspoon grated galangal
1 teaspoon grated turmeric or a pinch of ground turmeric
1 teaspoon shrimp paste

175 g (6 oz) skinless white fish fillets
3 tablespoons tamarind purée
175 g (6 oz) water spinach, cut into pieces,
  leaves separated
1 tablespoon fish sauce
1 tablespoon sugar

To make the sour curry paste, use a pestle and mortar or food processor to pound or blend all the ingredients together until smooth.

Remove any remaining bones from the fish using a pair of tweezers, then cut the fish fillets into 5 cm (2 in) pieces.

Bring 625 ml (22 fl oz/2½ cups) water to the boil in a saucepan. Stir in the curry paste and reduce the heat to medium. Add the tamarind, water spinach stems, fish sauce and sugar and cook for 2–3 minutes. Add the fish and cook for 1–2 minutes. Add the water spinach leaves and adjust the seasoning. Serve hot with rice.

PICTURE ON PAGE 58

SERVES 4

KHAO TOM PLAA
Rice Soup with Fish Fillets

2 tablespoons vegetable oil
3–4 large garlic cloves, finely chopped
1.25 litres (44 fl oz/5 cups) vegetable or fish stock
2½ tablespoons light soy sauce
2 teaspoons preserved radish, sliced
245 g (9 oz/1⅓ cups) cooked jasmine rice

280 g (10 oz) skinless white fish fillets, cut into
  bite-sized pieces
1 tablespoon finely sliced ginger
1 spring onion (scallion), finely chopped, for garnish
a few coriander (cilantro) leaves, for garnish
ground white pepper, for sprinkling

Heat the oil in a small wok or frying pan and stir-fry the garlic until light golden. Remove from the heat and discard the garlic.

Heat the stock to boiling point in a saucepan. Add the light soy sauce, preserved radish and rice and cook over medium heat for 2–3 minutes. Add the

fish and ginger and cook for another 1–2 minutes, or until the fish is cooked. Season well, taste, then adjust the seasoning again if necessary.

Garnish with spring onion and coriander leaves and sprinkle with ground pepper and the garlic oil.

SERVES 4

Sour Fish Soup with Water Spinach
(recipe on page 57)

Kaeng Jeut Wun Sen Muu Sap
Vermicelli Soup with Minced Pork

This is a light, clear soup from the north of Thailand. Unlike other noodle recipes, this one is always eaten with rice. It is a warming 'comfort food' and is very easy to prepare. The noodles continue to soak up liquid as they sit, so serve the soup straight away.

15 pieces of dried black fungus
50 g (2 oz) mung bean vermicelli
2 tablespoons vegetable oil
3–4 large garlic cloves, finely chopped
450 g (1 lb) minced (ground) pork
20 coriander (cilantro) leaves, finely chopped

$1/4$ teaspoon salt
$1/4$ teaspoon ground white pepper
625 ml (22 fl oz/$2^{1}/2$ cups) vegetable or chicken stock
2 tablespoons light soy sauce
1 tablespoon preserved radish
a few coriander (cilantro) leaves, for garnish

Soak the mushrooms in hot water for 5 minutes, or until soft, then drain them and cut into smaller pieces if necessary.

Soak the mung bean vermicelli in hot water for 5–7 minutes, or until soft, then drain it well and cut it into small pieces.

Heat the oil in a small wok or frying pan and stir-fry the chopped garlic until light golden. Remove from the heat, lift out the garlic with a slotted spoon and drain on paper towels.

In a bowl, combine the pork with the coriander leaves, salt and pepper. Use a spoon or your wet hands to shape the mixture into small balls about 1 cm ($1/2$ in) in diameter.

Heat the stock to boiling point in a saucepan. Add the light soy sauce and radish. Lower the pork balls into the stock and cook for 2 minutes over medium heat. Add the mushrooms and the noodles and cook for 1–2 minutes, stirring frequently. Taste, then adjust the seasoning and sprinkle with the garlic, garlic oil and coriander.

SERVES 4

KAENG JEUT PLAA MEUK SAI MUU

Stuffed Squid Soup

Kaeng jeut are one of the three main types of soup commonly found in Thailand. The name means bland soup. These soups are not highly flavoured so you should use the best-quality stock possible.

280 g (10 oz) small squid
2 coriander (cilantro) roots, finely chopped
3–4 large garlic cloves, roughly chopped
280 g (10 oz) minced (ground) pork or chicken
1/4 teaspoon salt
1/4 teaspoon ground white pepper
2 litres (70 fl oz/8 cups) vegetable stock

2.5 cm (1 in) piece of ginger, sliced
80 ml (3 fl oz/1/3 cup) light soy sauce
1 tablespoon preserved radish, sliced
5 spring onions (scallions), slivered, for garnish
a few coriander (cilantro) leaves, for garnish
ground white pepper, for sprinkling

To clean each squid, grasp the body in one hand and pull away the head and tentacles from the body. Cut the head off the tentacles just above the eyes and discard the head. Clean out the body. Pull the skin off the squid and rinse well. Drain well.

Using a pestle and mortar, pound the coriander roots and garlic into a paste. Combine the paste with the pork or chicken and the salt and pepper in a bowl. Spoon some mixture into a squid sac until two-thirds full, being careful not to overfill it as the filling will swell during cooking. Squeeze the squid tube closed at the end and seal with a sharp toothpick. Prick several holes in the body

of the squid. Place on a plate and repeat with the rest of the squid. Use a spoon or your wet fingers to shape the remaining meat mixture into small balls about 1 cm (1/2 in) in diameter.

Heat the stock to boiling point in a saucepan. Reduce the heat to low and add the ginger, light soy sauce and radish. Lower the meatballs into the stock, then gently drop in the stuffed squid and cook over low heat for 4–5 minutes, or until the meatballs and squid are cooked. Taste the broth and adjust the seasoning if necessary. Garnish with the spring onions and coriander leaves, and sprinkle with ground white pepper.

SERVES 4

Far left: Spoon the pork mixture into the squid sacs, being careful not to overfill them.

Left: Use a sharp toothpick to seal the squid tube closed.

Tom Khaa Kai

Chicken, Coconut and Galangal Soup

This is one of the classic soups of Thailand. The Thai name means 'boiled galangal chicken'. Although usually made with chicken, you can make this recipe using prawns, fish or vegetables. Don't worry when the coconut milk splits – it is supposed to.

750 ml (27 fl oz/3 cups) coconut milk (page 245)
2 lemon grass stalks, white part only, each cut into
  a tassel or bruised
5 cm (2 in) piece of galangal, cut into several pieces
4 Asian shallots, smashed with the flat side of a cleaver
400 g (14 oz) boneless, skinless chicken breast, sliced
2 tablespoons fish sauce
1 tablespoon palm sugar (jaggery)

200 g (7 oz) baby tomatoes, cut into bite-sized pieces
  if large
150 g (6 oz) straw mushrooms or button mushrooms
3 tablespoons lime juice
6 makrut (kaffir) lime leaves, torn in half
3–5 bird's eye chillies, stems removed, bruised, or
  2 long red chillies, seeded and finely sliced
a few coriander (cilantro) leaves, for garnish

Put the coconut milk, lemon grass, galangal and shallots in a saucepan or wok over medium heat and bring to the boil.

Add the chicken, fish sauce and palm sugar and simmer, stirring constantly for 5 minutes, or until the chicken is cooked through.

Add the tomatoes and mushrooms and simmer for 2–3 minutes. Add the lime juice, lime leaves and chillies in the last few seconds, taking care not to let the tomatoes lose their shape. Taste, then adjust the seasoning if necessary. This dish is not meant to be overwhelmingly hot, but to have a sweet, salty, sour taste. Garnish with coriander leaves.

SERVES 4

It is best to carefully measure ingredients such as fish sauce as the flavour is quite strong.

Khao Tom Kung Lae Kai

Rice Soup with Prawns and Chicken

Although derived from Chinese-style congee, Thai rice soups use whole rice grains rather than the broken grains preferred by the Chinese. Rice soups are enjoyed as a snack at night or as a breakfast dish. They are sustaining enough to be a meal.

110 g (4 oz) raw prawns (shrimp)
2 tablespoons vegetable oil
3–4 large garlic cloves, finely chopped
1 coriander (cilantro) root, finely chopped
1 garlic clove, extra, roughly chopped
a pinch of ground white pepper, plus extra, to sprinkle
75 g (3 oz) minced (ground) chicken or pork
1 spring onion (scallion), finely chopped

935 ml (33 fl oz/3¾ cups) chicken or vegetable stock
2 tablespoons light soy sauce
2 teaspoons preserved radish
325 g (11 oz/1¾ cups) cooked jasmine rice
1 tablespoon thinly sliced ginger
1 Chinese cabbage leaf, roughly chopped
2 spring onions (scallions), finely chopped, for garnish
a few coriander (cilantro) leaves, for garnish

Peel and devein the prawns and cut each prawn along the back so it opens like a butterfly (leave each prawn joined along the base and at the tail, leaving the tail attached).

Heat the oil in a small wok or frying pan and stir-fry the finely chopped garlic until light golden. Remove from the heat and discard the garlic.

Using a pestle and mortar or a small blender, pound or blend the coriander root, roughly chopped garlic, pepper and a pinch of salt into a paste. In a bowl, combine the coriander paste with the chicken or pork and spring onion. Using

a spoon or your wet hands, shape the mixture into small balls about 1 cm (½ in) in diameter.

Heat the stock to boiling point in a saucepan. Add the light soy sauce, preserved radish and rice. Lower the meatballs into the stock over medium heat and cook for 3 minutes, or until the chicken is cooked. Add the prawns, ginger and Chinese cabbage to the stock. Cook for 1–2 minutes, or until the prawns open and turn pink. Taste, then adjust the seasoning if necessary. Garnish with spring onions and coriander leaves. Sprinkle with ground white pepper and the garlic oil.

SERVES 4

The delicious flavour of this soup comes from the melding of prawns, chicken and vegetables.

Chapter 3

SALADS

Fresh, crisp vegetables, mostly raw but sometimes lightly cooked, feature in salads that also include fresh fruit, spices and herbs. Sweet tastes are paired with sour in a balancing act of exhilarating intensity.

Yam Kai

Chicken and Papaya Salad

One of Thailand's many hot and tangy salads, this version has coconut rice included, but you could serve it on its own if you prefer. Make sure the papaya is green, and not ripe, or the salad won't taste at all right.

250 ml (9 fl oz/1 cup) coconut cream (page 245)

200 g (7 oz) boneless, skinless chicken breast, trimmed

200 g (7 oz/1 cup) jasmine rice

350 ml (12 fl oz/1⅓ cups) coconut milk (page 245)

2 garlic cloves, chopped

3 Asian shallots, chopped

3 small red chillies

1 teaspoon small dried shrimp

2 tablespoons fish sauce

8 cherry tomatoes, cut in halves

150 g (6 oz) green papaya, grated

2 tablespoons lime juice

30 g (1 oz/1½ cups) mint leaves, roughly chopped

20 g (1 oz/⅔ cup) coriander (cilantro) leaves, roughly chopped

Bring the coconut cream to the boil in a small saucepan. Add the chicken and simmer over low heat for 5 minutes. Turn off the heat and cover the pan for 20 minutes. Remove the chicken from the pan and shred it.

Wash the rice under cold running water until the water runs clear. Put the rice and coconut milk in a small saucepan and bring to the boil. Reduce the heat to low, cover the pan with a tight-fitting lid and simmer for 20 minutes. Remove from the heat and leave the lid on until ready to serve.

Using a pestle and mortar or blender, pound or blend the garlic, shallots and chillies together. Add the shrimp and fish sauce and pound to break up the dried shrimp. Add the tomatoes and pound all the ingredients together to form a rough paste.

In a bowl, combine the shredded chicken and chilli paste mixture with the grated papaya, lime juice, mint and coriander leaves. Serve with the hot coconut rice.

SERVES 4

Pound the chilli paste ingredients together in a pestle and mortar, or if you prefer, use a blender.

Yam Neua Yang Nahm Toke

Sliced Steak with Hot and Sour Sauce

Yam Neua Yang Nahm Toke literally means 'beef grilled on burning hot charcoal until the juices fall'. This northern salad is eaten with sticky rice and is perfect with beer, Thai whisky or wine. Serve the salad with raw vegetables such as green cabbage.

350 g (12 oz) lean sirloin, rump or fillet steak
2 tablespoons fish sauce
4 tablespoons lime juice
1 teaspoon sugar
¼ teaspoon roasted chilli powder
3–4 Asian shallots, thinly sliced

a few lettuce leaves, to serve
20 g (1 oz/⅓ cup) roughly chopped coriander (cilantro) leaves, for garnish
15 g (½ oz/¼ cup) roughly chopped mint leaves, for garnish

Heat a barbecue or a grill (broiler) to medium. If using a grill, line the tray with foil. Put the beef on the grill rack and sprinkle both sides with salt and pepper. Cook for 5–7 minutes on each side, turning occasionally. Fat should drip off the meat and the meat should cook slowly enough to remain juicy and not burn. Using a sharp knife, slice the cooked beef crossways into strips.

Mix the fish sauce, lime juice, sugar and roasted chilli powder in a bowl. Add the Asian shallots and the beef slices. Taste, then adjust the seasoning if necessary.

Line a serving plate with lettuce leaves, then spoon the beef mixture over the leaves. Sprinkle with the coriander and mint leaves.

SERVES 4

Heat the barbecue to medium before adding the meat.

YAM SOM OH

Prawn and Pomelo Salad

This northern Thai salad uses pomelo to give it a sweet/tart flavour. Different varieties of pomelo are available in Thailand: some have pink flesh and others have yellow. Serve the salad with sticky rice and eat it as soon as it is ready.

1 large pomelo
1 tablespoon fish sauce
1 tablespoon lime juice
1 teaspoon sugar
1 tablespoon chilli jam (page 240)
300 g (11 oz) raw medium prawns (shrimp), peeled and deveined, tails intact
3 tablespoons shredded fresh coconut, lightly toasted until golden (if fresh is unavailable, use shredded desiccated coconut)

3 Asian shallots, thinly sliced
5 bird's eye chillies, bruised
20 g (1 oz/1 cup) mint leaves
10 g (1/2 oz/1/3 cup) coriander (cilantro) leaves
1 tablespoon fried Asian shallots

To peel a pomelo, slice a circular patch off the top of the fruit, about 2 cm (3/4 in) deep. Next, score four deep lines from top to bottom, dividing the skin into four segments. Peel it away, one quarter at a time. Remove any remaining pith and separate the segments of the fruit. Peel the segments and remove any visible seeds. Crumble the segments into their component parts, without squashing them or releasing the juice.

To make the dressing, combine the fish sauce, lime juice, sugar and chilli jam in a small bowl.

Bring a large saucepan of water to the boil. Add the prawns and cook for 2 minutes. Drain and allow the prawns to cool.

In a large bowl, gently combine the pomelo pieces, prawns, toasted coconut, shallots, chillies, mint and coriander. Just before serving, add the dressing. Toss gently to combine and coat the ingredients. Serve sprinkled with fried shallots.

SERVES 4

Slice off a section from the top of the pomelo before cutting it into sections and segmenting it.

YAM PUU MAMUANG
Crab and Green Mango Salad

2 tablespoons fish sauce
2 tablespoons lime juice
2 teaspoons palm sugar (jaggery)
2 green bird's eye chillies, chopped
2 red bird's eye chillies, chopped
1 teaspoon ground dried shrimp
300 g (11 oz) fresh crab meat

30 g (1 oz/^{2}/$_3$ cup) chopped mint leaves
20 g (1 oz/^{1}/$_3$ cup) chopped coriander (cilantro) leaves
4 Asian shallots, thinly sliced
1 green mango, flesh finely shredded
1 tomato, cut in half lengthways and thinly sliced
1 large green chilli, thinly sliced on an angle

To make a dressing, put the fish sauce, lime juice, palm sugar, bird's eye chillies and dried shrimp in a small bowl and stir to dissolve the sugar.

Just before serving, put the crab meat, mint and coriander leaves, shallots, mango and tomato in a large bowl and toss gently. Pour the dressing over the salad, then toss to combine and serve with the sliced chilli on top.

SERVES 4

YAM PLAA YAANG
Hot and Sour Grilled Fish Salad

2 mackerel or whiting (about 400 g/14 oz each fish), cleaned and gutted, with or without head, or firm white fish fillets
2 lemon grass stalks, white part only, thinly sliced
2 Asian shallots, thinly sliced
1 spring onion (scallion), thinly sliced
2.5 cm (1 in) piece of ginger, thinly sliced

5 makrut (kaffir) lime leaves, thinly sliced
20 g (1 oz/1 cup) mint leaves
100 ml (4 fl oz) lime juice
1 tablespoon fish sauce
4–5 bird's eye chillies, thinly sliced
a few lettuce leaves
1 long red chilli, seeded and thinly sliced, for garnish

Heat a barbecue or a grill (broiler) to medium. If using a grill, line the tray with foil. Cook the fish for about 20 minutes on each side, or until the fish is cooked and light brown.

Use your hands to remove the fish heads, backbone and other bones. Break the fish, including the skin, into bite-sized chunks and put them in a bowl. Add the lemon grass, shallots, spring onion, ginger, lime leaves, mint leaves, lime juice, fish sauce and chillies. Mix well, then adjust the seasoning.

Line a serving plate with lettuce leaves, then spoon the salad over the leaves. Sprinkle with chilli slices.

SERVES 4

Laap Pet

Spicy Ground Duck

Laap means 'good fortune'. This version using duck is a speciality from around Ubon Rachathani but you can use minced chicken instead of duck. Laap is served with raw vegetables such as snake beans, cabbage and firm, crisp lettuce.

1 tablespoon jasmine rice
280 g (10 oz) minced (ground) duck
3 tablespoons lime juice
1 tablespoon fish sauce
2 lemon grass stalks, white part only, thinly sliced
50 g (2 oz) Asian shallots, thinly sliced
5 makrut (kaffir) lime leaves, thinly sliced

5 spring onions (scallions), finely chopped
1/4–1/2 teaspoon roasted chilli powder, according to taste
a few lettuce leaves
a few mint leaves, for garnish
raw vegetables such as snake (yard-long) beans, cut into lengths, cucumber slices, thin wedges of cabbage, halved baby tomatoes, to serve

Dry-fry the rice in a small pan over medium heat. Shake the pan to move the rice around for 6–8 minutes, or until the rice is brown. Using a pestle and mortar or a small blender, pound or blend the rice until it almost forms a powder.

In a saucepan or wok, cook the duck with the lime juice and fish sauce over high heat. Crumble and break the duck until the meat has separated into small pieces. Cook until light brown and dry, then remove from the heat.

Add the rice powder, lemon grass, shallots, lime leaves, spring onions and chilli powder to the duck and stir together. Taste, then adjust the seasoning if necessary.

Line a serving plate with lettuce leaves. Spoon the duck over the leaves, then garnish with mint leaves. Arrange the vegetables on a separate plate.

SERVES 4

Pound the dry-fried rice in a pestle and mortar until it forms a powder. Alternatively, you can use a small blender.

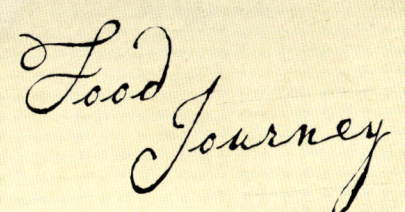

FRUIT

⬦⬦⬦⬦⬦⬦⬦⬦⬦⬦⬦⬦⬦⬦⬦⬦⬦⬦⬦⬦⬦⬦⬦⬦⬦

A wonderful array of tropical fruit is taken for granted as part of everyday life in Thailand. Fruit is eaten at breakfast, as a snack, instead of dessert, and appears in many recipes. It is also juiced, dried, pickled and salted. It is sold on every street corner of every city, town and village.

Tropical fruit grows well throughout Thailand. A drive around the countryside reveals rows of fruit trees, and not just in orchards. Even in town, every spare scrap of land has a banana tree or two, a papaya tree and possibly even a mango tree. Fresh fruit is often sold prepared. You can buy a plastic bag full of fruit pieces with a wooden skewer for picking them up. Most bags come with a little bag of seasoning. Thais like a balance of flavours and fruit is no exception. Salt, sugar and a little chilli powder perk up fruit and bring out the flavour.

Fruit is used extensively in Thai cuisine. Jackfruit, carambola (starfruit), mangosteen, green mango and lychees are all used in curries. Salads are made from green mango, papaya or pieces of pomelo. Bananas are steamed in their skins and served for breakfast, or speared on skewers and roasted over hot coals to be eaten as a roadside snack. Desserts include the ubiquitous banana fritters, as well as bananas simmered in coconut milk, sticky rice with mango, macerated fruit and grilled bananas. Modern cuisine has embraced ice creams and sorbets made in every imaginable fruit flavour.

Fresh fruit juices (naam pan) often come as something of a shock to the visitor to Thailand. Just as fresh fruit is eaten with a special seasoning of chilli, sugar and salt, fruit juices are 'seasoned' with salt. Juices usually consist of chopped fruit, water and ice blended with a pinch of salt.

In Thailand, as many types of fruit as possible are preserved by dry-salting, pickling, candying or drying. Bags of preserved fruit are sold at stalls and are as common as bags of sweets in the West.

The infamous durian is the most anticipated fruit in the Thai calendar. Although 'tasting like heaven but smelling like hell', durian has a reputation second to none. The putrid smell lingers but is not enough to deter enthusiasts from loving the rich pulp. Different varieties are available throughout the year but, when not in season, a desire for it can be satisfied by products such as freeze-dried chips or deep-fried slices.

Bananas, guavas, jackfruit, limes, watermelons, oranges, papayas, pomelos and pineapples are always present. European fruit is now grown in the cooler uplands. Orchards of peaches, cherries and apples, as well as hothouses with strawberries growing, are seen alongside lychees.

March sees the arrival of mangoes, followed by mangosteens in April and lychees in May. The following five months are the best time for fruit: custard apples, longans, rambutans, rose apples, sapodilla, carambola, jujube, langsat, santol and sala come into season and then go again.

Yam Plaa

Crispy Fish Salad

The fish (traditionally catfish) in this recipe is turned into an almost unrecognizable fluffy, crunchy affair that is then flavoured with a sweet, hot and sour dressing. Pink salmon is suitable to use as a substitute for the white fish.

300 g (11 oz) skinless firm white fish fillets

1 tablespoon sea salt

peanut oil, for deep-frying

3 tomatoes or large cherry tomatoes, each cut into 4 or 6 wedges

2 Asian shallots, thinly sliced

1 small red onion, sliced into thin wedges

15 g (½ oz/½ cup) coriander (cilantro) leaves

18–24 mint leaves

2 tablespoons roasted peanuts, roughly chopped

DRESSING

1 lemon grass stalk, white part only, roughly chopped

4 bird's eye chillies, stems removed

1 garlic clove, chopped

1 tablespoon fish sauce

2 tablespoons lime juice

2 teaspoons palm sugar (jaggery)

¼ teaspoon ground turmeric

Preheat the oven to 180°C (350°F/Gas 4). Pat dry the fish fillets, then toss them in the sea salt. Place on a rack in a baking tray and bake for 20 minutes.

To make the dressing, use a pestle and mortar or a food processor to pound or blend the lemon grass, chillies and garlic to a paste. Transfer to a small bowl and add the fish sauce, lime juice, sugar and turmeric. Stir until the sugar dissolves.

Transfer the cooled fish to a food processor and chop until it resembles large breadcrumbs.

Half fill a wok with oil and heat over high heat. Drop a small piece of fish into the oil. If it sizzles immediately, the oil is ready. Drop a large handful of the chopped fish into the hot oil. The fish will puff up and turn crisp. Cook for 30 seconds and carefully stir a little. Cook for another 30 seconds, or until golden brown. Remove with a slotted spoon and drain on paper towels. Repeat to cook all the fish.

Put the tomatoes, shallots, red onion, coriander leaves, mint leaves and peanuts in a bowl with about half of the dressing. Transfer the salad to a serving plate. Break the fish into smaller pieces if you wish and place on the salad. To ensure that the fish stays crisp, pour the remaining dressing over the salad just before serving.

SERVES 4

Yam Wun Sen Thaleh

Hot and Sour Vermicelli with Mixed Seafood

One of the milder classic salads found all over Thailand, often made just with prawns, but here made with seafood. The vermicelli becomes almost translucent when soaked. As the dressing is absorbed quickly, don't make the salad too far ahead.

110 g (4 oz) mung bean vermicelli
175 g (6 oz) mixed raw medium prawns (shrimp), squid tubes and scallops
8 mussels
15 g (½ oz) dried black fungus (about half a handful)
1½ tablespoons vegetable oil
4–5 garlic cloves, finely chopped
3 tablespoons lime juice

1 tablespoon fish sauce
2 lemon grass stalks, white part only, thinly sliced
3 Asian shallots, thinly sliced
¼–½ teaspoon chilli powder or 2–3 bird's eye chillies, thinly sliced
3 spring onions (scallions), finely chopped
a few lettuce leaves
1 long red chilli, seeded and thinly sliced, for garnish

Soak the mung bean vermicelli in boiling water for 1–2 minutes, or until soft, then drain and roughly chop the noodles.

Peel and devein the prawns and cut each prawn along the back so it opens like a butterfly (leave each prawn joined along the base and at the tail, leaving the tail attached).

Peel off the skin from the squid tubes, rinse the insides and cut the tubes into 5 mm (¼ in) rings. Remove any dark veins from the scallops.

Scrub the mussels and remove their hairy beards. Discard any open mussels and any that don't close when tapped on the work surface.

Soak the fungus in boiling water for 2–3 minutes, or until soft, then drain and roughly chop.

Heat the oil in a small wok or frying pan and stir the garlic over medium heat until light brown. Transfer the fried garlic to a small bowl.

Cook the prawns, squid rings and mussels in a saucepan or wok over medium heat with the lime juice and fish sauce for 1–2 minutes, or until the prawns open and turn pink. Add the scallops and cook for 1 minute. Discard any unopened mussels. Add the vermicelli and chopped black fungus and cook for 2 minutes, or until the vermicelli is cooked. Remove from the heat. Add the lemon grass, shallots, chilli powder or chillies, and spring onions and mix well. Taste, then adjust the seasoning if necessary.

Line a serving plate with lettuce leaves, then spoon the seafood over the leaves. Sprinkle with chilli slices and the fried garlic.

SERVES 4

Chapter 4

FISH AND SHELLFISH

Steamed or grilled, roasted whole in banana leaves, stir-fried, dried or pickled: there's a cooking method suitable for each of the many species of fish and shellfish plucked from coastal waters and rivers.

PLA THAWT BAI HOHRAPHAA
Deep-fried Fish with Chillies and Basil

This is one of the most popular fish dishes in Thailand and you can use most types of fish to make it. The fish has a mildly spicy flavour and is garnished with deep-fried chilli and basil leaves. The dusting of flour isn't traditional but it helps crisp the skin.

1 large or 2 smaller red snapper (total weight about 1 kg/2 lb 4 oz)
3 tablespoons plain (all-purpose) flour
pinch of ground black pepper
1½ tablespoons vegetable oil
½ tablespoon red curry paste (page 236) or bought paste

2 tablespoons palm sugar (jaggery)
2 tablespoons fish sauce
vegetable oil, for deep-frying
a handful of Thai sweet basil leaves
1 dried long red chilli, cut into 5 mm (¼ in) pieces, seeds discarded
3 makrut (kaffir) lime leaves, very thinly sliced, for garnish

Clean and gut the snapper, leaving the head on. Thoroughly dry the fish and score it three or four times on both sides with a sharp knife. Rub it inside and out with a pinch of salt. Place the flour and pepper on a plate and press the fish lightly into it until coated with flour from head to tail. Shake off any excess.

Heat the oil in a small saucepan, add the red curry paste and stir over medium heat for 1–2 minutes, or until fragrant. Add the palm sugar, fish sauce and 2 tablespoons water and cook for 1–2 minutes, or until the sugar has dissolved. Remove the pan from the heat.

Heat 10 cm (4 in) oil in a large wok or pan large enough to deep-fry the whole fish. When the oil is hot, drop a few basil leaves into it. If they sizzle immediately, the oil is ready. Deep-fry half of the basil leaves for 1 minute, or until crisp. Remove with a slotted spoon and drain on paper towels. Deep-fry the rest.

In the same wok, deep-fry the dried chilli pieces for a few seconds until light brown. Be careful not to burn them. Remove with a slotted spoon and drain on paper towels. Lower the heat to medium and gently slide the fish into the oil. Be careful as the hot oil may splash. Deep-fry the fish on just one side (but make sure the oil covers the whole fish) for 5–10 minutes, or until the fish is cooked and light brown (if you cook the fish until it is very brown, it will be too dry). Drain off the oil and drain the fish on paper towels.

Put the curry sauce in the wok and gently warm it. Add the fried fish and coat both sides with the sauce. Transfer the fish to a warm plate with any remaining sauce and sprinkle with the crisp basil, fried chilli pieces and makrut lime leaves.

SERVES 4

Haw Mok Thaleh Phrik Yuak
Curried Fish Steamed in Banana Chillies

A smooth curried custard with fish fills these chillies. Choose a selection of colours for a very striking dish. Red, yellow and orange chillies keep their colour better than green ones. You can also use small capsicums of various colours.

FISH FILLING
4–5 dried long red chillies
3 garlic cloves, roughly chopped
1–2 Asian shallots, roughly chopped
4 coriander (cilantro) roots, roughly chopped
1 lemon grass stalk, white part only, thinly sliced
1 cm (1/2 in) piece of galangal, finely chopped
1 teaspoon makrut (kaffir) lime zest or 2 makrut (kaffir) lime leaves, finely sliced
1 teaspoon shrimp paste
1/4 teaspoon salt
275 g (10 oz) firm white fish fillets, cut into 1 cm (1/2 in) pieces, or small raw prawns (shrimp) or small scallops

400 ml (14 fl oz/1 2/3 cups) coconut milk (page 245)
2 eggs
2 tablespoons fish sauce

10 banana chillies, or small capsicums (peppers), preferably elongated ones
2 handfuls of Thai sweet basil leaves
2 tablespoons coconut cream (page 245)
3–4 makrut (kaffir) lime leaves, thinly sliced, for garnish
1 long red chilli, seeded, thinly sliced, for garnish

To make the fish filling, using a pestle and mortar or blender, pound or blend the chillies, garlic, shallots and coriander roots together. Add the lemon grass, galangal, makrut lime zest, shrimp paste and salt, one ingredient at a time, until the mixture forms a paste.

In a bowl, combine the curry paste, fish, coconut milk, eggs and fish sauce. Keep stirring in the same direction for 10 minutes, then cover and refrigerate for 30 minutes to set slightly.

If using chillies, or if the capsicums are the long ones, make a long cut with a sharp knife, or if they are the round ones, cut a small round slice from the tops. Remove the seeds and membrane, then clean the chillies or capsicums and pat them dry. Place a few basil leaves in the bottom of each.

Spoon in the fish mixture until it nearly reaches the top edge.

Fill a wok or a steamer pan with water, cover and bring to a rolling boil over high heat. Place the chillies or capsicums on a plate. Use a plate that will fit on the rack of a traditional bamboo steamer basket or on a steamer rack inside the wok or pan. Taking care not to burn your hands, set the basket or rack over the water and put the plate on the rack. Reduce the heat to a simmer. Cover and cook for 15–20 minutes. Check and replenish the water after 10 minutes.

Turn off the heat and transfer the chillies or capsicums to a serving plate. Spoon the coconut cream on top and sprinkle with makrut lime leaves and sliced chilli.

SERVES 4

Neung Hawy Lai Kra-Chai
Clams and Mussels with Chinese Keys

450 g (1 lb) mixed clams and mussels in the shell
75 g (3 oz) Chinese keys, thinly sliced
2.5 cm (1 in) piece of galangal, cut into 7–8 slices
1 long red chilli, seeded and finely chopped

2 teaspoons fish sauce
1/2 teaspoon sugar
a few sprigs of basil leaves, for garnish

Scrub the clams and mussels and remove any hairy beards from the mussels. Discard any open mussels or clams and any that don't close when tapped on the work surface. Wash them all in several changes of cold water until the water is clear, then put them in a large bowl, cover with cold water and soak for 30 minutes. This helps remove the sand.

Put the clams and mussels, Chinese keys, galangal and chilli in a large saucepan or wok. Cover loosely and cook over medium heat for 5 minutes, shaking the pan frequently. Add the fish sauce and sugar and toss together. Discard any unopened shells. Serve the clams and mussels in a large bowl, garnished with basil leaves.

PICTURE ON OPPOSITE PAGE

SERVES 2

Phat Hawy Malaeng Phuu Ta-Khrai
Mussels with Lemon Grass

450 g (1 lb) mussels or clams in the shell
1 1/2 tablespoons vegetable oil
2–3 garlic cloves, finely chopped
1 small onion, finely chopped
3 lemon grass stalks, white part only, thinly sliced
2.5 cm (1 in) piece of galangal, cut into 7–8 slices

2 long red chillies, seeded and finely chopped
1 tablespoon fish sauce
1 tablespoon lime juice
1/2 teaspoon sugar
25 g (1 oz/1 cup) holy basil leaves, roughly chopped

Scrub the mussels or clams and remove any hairy beards from the mussels. Discard any open mussels or clams and any that don't close when tapped on the work surface. If using clams, wash them in several changes of cold water until the water is clear, then put them in a large bowl, cover with water and soak for 30 minutes to remove the sand.

Heat the oil in a wok and stir-fry the garlic, onion, lemon grass, galangal and chillies over medium

heat for 1–2 minutes, or until fragrant. Add the mussels or clams and stir-fry for a few minutes.

Add the fish sauce, lime juice and sugar. Cover loosely and cook for 5–7 minutes, shaking the wok frequently. Cook until the shells are open, discarding any unopened shells. Mix in the holy basil. Taste, then adjust the seasoning if necessary. Serve hot.

SERVES 2

FISH AND SEAFOOD

Freshwater fish and seafood are an integral part of the Thai diet. As a food they are second only to rice in importance. While fresh seafood is eaten by most people on an almost daily basis, fish sauce and shrimp paste are also part of the Thai lexicon of flavourings used in virtually every dish.

Fish and seafood are caught all over Thailand, along the 2710 kilometres (1685 miles) of coastline, from lakes, inland waterways, ponds and even in amongst rice paddies and in puddles left after storms. Fishing is done by commercial boats, communities and individuals. Wholesale markets at every major port send the catch both abroad and to markets throughout Thailand. Inland, fish is likely to be local freshwater fish, sold at markets with only a tiny amount on offer. Fish caught locally tend to be sold locally, unless they are caught commercially.

The fish market at Ranong deals both in fish caught locally and those found further out to sea. At smaller markets, fresh fish is sold just caught, or even still alive, from buckets and tanks. Market vendors kill and clean the fish as it is sold. Most fish are cooked with the head still on and the cheeks of the fish are considered to be the tastiest parts. Prawns and shrimp are very popular: tiger prawns are farmed on a large scale and are particularly meaty.

The majority of what comes out of Thailand's water is dried, preserved or converted to shrimp paste and fish sauce. The sun is used to dry fish, shrimp and squid all along the coast, spread out on mats or on bamboo frames. Fish, crabs and shellfish such as mussels are also pickled. Small amounts of preserved or dried fish add lots of flavour and can be used to dress rice or vegetables. Shrimp paste forms the base of dips eaten with fresh vegetables. Dried roast squid, a street snack, is the equivalent of a bag of chips. Small shrimp are dried and are either ground to a powder or soaked in a liquid before use.

Different areas have particular specialities and marine-based industries. People make their own fish sauce, but commercial operations can be found on the Gulf of Thailand. The Isthmus of Kra and islands are famous for fresh fish and shellfish, grilled (broiled) or barbecued, and Pattaya for crayfish. Inland, during April and May, giant catfish are fished from the Mekong in the North. Prawns are farmed in mangroves, though often not to the benefit of the environment or locals.

PLAA PHAO

Grilled Fish with Garlic and Coriander

Banana leaves are used in this recipe to protect the fish from direct heat as well as to add a subtle extra flavour. The leaves will char as they cook. You will find banana leaves in Asian supermarkets, often in the freezer cabinets.

4 red tilapa, grey/red mullet, or mackerel
    (about 300 g/11 oz each)
8–10 garlic cloves, roughly chopped
6 coriander (cilantro) roots, chopped
1 teaspoon ground white pepper

1 teaspoon salt
1 tablespoon vegetable oil
8 pieces of banana leaf
a chilli sauce, to serve

Clean and gut the fish, leaving the heads on. Dry the fish thoroughly. Score each fish three or four times on both sides with a sharp knife.

Using a pestle and mortar or small blender, pound or blend the garlic, coriander roots, pepper, salt and oil into a paste. Rub the garlic paste inside the cavities and all over each fish. Cover and marinate in the refrigerator for at least 30 minutes.

To soften the banana leaves and prevent them from splitting, put them in a hot oven for about 10–20 seconds, or blanch them briefly. Using two pieces of banana leaf, each with the grain running at right angles to the other, wrap each fish like a parcel. Pin the ends of the banana leaves together with toothpicks.

Heat a grill (broiler) or barbecue to medium. Barbecue or grill (broil) the fish for 15 minutes on each side, or until the fish is light brown and cooked. To make the fish easier to lift and turn during cooking, you can place the fish in a fish-shaped griddle that opens out like tongs. Transfer the fish to a serving plate. Serve with a chilli sauce.

SERVES 4

Right: Score the fish on both sides with a sharp knife.

Far right: Rub the garlic paste all over the fish and inside the cavities, then wrap it in the banana leaves.

PUU PHAT PHONG KARII

Cracked Crab with Curry Powder

This crab recipe is one of the few Thai dishes to use curry powder as a main flavouring. Bought curry powder (look for a Thai brand) is usually very good and this is what Thai cooks use, but there is a recipe on page 243 if you need to make your own.

1 live crab, 500 g (1 lb 2 oz)
170 ml (6 fl oz/²⁄₃ cup) coconut milk (page 245)
1 tablespoon light soy sauce
½ tablespoon oyster sauce
2 teaspoons Thai curry powder (page 243) or bought
 Thai curry powder
¼ teaspoon sugar

2 tablespoons vegetable oil
3–4 garlic cloves, finely chopped
1 small onion, cut into 3 wedges
2 spring onions (scallions), thinly sliced
½ long red chilli, seeded and thinly sliced, for garnish
a few coriander (cilantro) leaves, for garnish

Put the crabs in the freezer for 1 hour. Leaving the legs attached, cut the crab in half through the centre of the shell from head to rear. Cut in half again from left to right (quartering the crab), with legs attached to each quarter. Twist off and remove the upper shell pieces. Discard the stomach sac and the soft gill tissue. Using crackers or the back of a heavy knife, crack the claws to make them easier to eat. If the claws are big, cut them in half.

Mix the coconut milk, light soy sauce, oyster sauce, curry powder and sugar in a bowl.

Heat the oil in a wok or frying pan. Stir-fry the garlic over medium heat until light brown. Add the crab and stir-fry for 4–5 minutes. Add the coconut mixture and onion and continue stir-frying for another 5–7 minutes, or until the crab meat is cooked through and the sauce is reduced and very thick. Add the spring onions. Taste, then adjust the seasoning if necessary. Spoon onto a serving plate and sprinkle with sliced chilli and coriander leaves.

SERVES 4

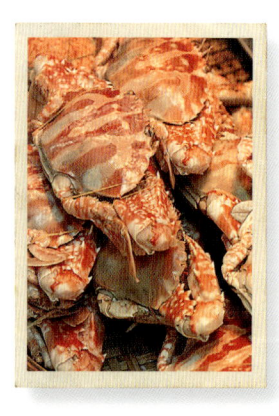 

Cut the crab into quarters, leaving the legs attached. Add the coconut milk mixture and onion after 5 minutes.

Plaa Thawt Sahm Rot

Deep-fried Fish with Three-flavoured Sauce

You can use lime juice in this dish if you prefer a clear sauce, or tamarind for a thick or darker-coloured sauce. Use two or four smaller fish if you can't find one fish large enough. Garnish with holy basil if you can find it.

1 x 350 g (12 oz) sea bream, red snapper or grey mullet
3 tablespoons plain (all-purpose) flour
pinch of ground black pepper
vegetable oil, for deep-frying
4–5 garlic cloves, roughly chopped
5 long red chillies, seeded and roughly chopped

4–5 Asian shallots, roughly chopped
3 coriander (cilantro) roots, finely chopped
3 tablespoons palm sugar (jaggery)
2 tablespoons fish sauce
3 tablespoons tamarind purée or lime juice
a few holy basil or Thai sweet basil leaves, for garnish

Clean and gut the fish, leaving the head on. Dry the fish thoroughly. Score the fish three times on both sides with a sharp knife. Rub the fish inside and out with a pinch of salt. Put the flour and ground pepper on a plate or dish and press the fish lightly into it until coated with flour from head to tail. Shake off any excess.

Heat 10 cm (4 in) oil in a large wok or pan big enough to deep-fry the whole fish. When the oil seems hot, drop in a piece of shallot. If it sizzles straight away, the oil is ready. Lower the heat to medium and gently slide the fish into the oil. Be careful as the hot oil may splash. Deep-fry the fish on one side (but make sure the oil covers the whole fish) for about 15–20 minutes, or until the fish is

cooked and light brown (if you cook the fish until it is brown, it will be too dry). Drain, then put on paper towels before transferring to a warm plate. Keep warm.

While the fish is cooking, use a pestle and mortar or a small blender to pound or blend the garlic, chillies, shallots and coriander roots together into a rough paste.

Heat 1 tablespoon oil in a wok or pan and stir-fry the chilli paste over medium heat for 2–3 minutes, or until fragrant. Add the sugar, fish sauce and tamarind or lime juice, and cook for 2–3 minutes, or until the sugar has dissolved. Pour the warm sauce over the fish and garnish with basil leaves.

SERVES 2

Far left: Coat the whole fish in seasoned flour.

Left: Deep-fry the fish on one side only, making sure the oil covers the fish.

PLAA NEUNG GEAM BOUI

Steamed Fish with Preserved Plum

Buy an appropriately large steamer for this recipe or use the steamer rack of your wok. Both will work equally well. Preserved plums are sold in jars in Asian supermarkets and, once opened, they will keep in the refrigerator for some time.

1 tablespoon light soy sauce

½ teaspoon sugar

1 large or 2 smaller pomfret, flounder, or turbot (total weight about 1 kg/2 lb 4 oz)

50 g (2 oz) mushrooms, roughly sliced

2 small preserved plums, bruised

5 cm (2 in) piece of ginger, julienned

4 spring onions (scallions), sliced diagonally

2 long red or green chillies, seeded and thinly sliced

a few coriander (cilantro) leaves, for garnish

a sprinkle of ground white pepper

In a small bowl, mix the light soy sauce and sugar.

Clean and gut the fish, leaving the head on. Dry the fish thoroughly. Score the fish three or four times on both sides with a sharp knife. Place the fish on a deep plate slightly larger than the fish. Use a plate that will fit on the rack of a traditional bamboo steamer basket or on a steamer rack inside the wok. Sprinkle the mushrooms, preserved plums and ginger over the fish. Pour the light soy sauce mixture all over the fish.

Fill a wok or a steamer pan with water, cover and bring to a rolling boil over high heat. Taking care not to burn your hands, set the rack or basket over the boiling water and put the plate with the fish on the rack. Reduce the heat to a simmer. Cover and steam for 25–30 minutes (depending on the size of the fish), or until a skewer will slide easily into the fish. Check and replenish the water every 10 minutes or so. Remove the plate and the fish from the steamer and sprinkle with the spring onions, chillies, coriander leaves and pepper.

SERVES 4

Haw Mok

Fish Steamed in Banana Leaf

The delicious aromatic curried fish custard filling for this dish is the same one as on page 93. In this recipe the fish custard is steamed in individual banana leaf cups and this results in a delightful exotic presentation.

banana leaves
2 handfuls of Thai sweet basil leaves
fish filling (page 93)

2 tablespoons coconut cream
3–4 makrut (kaffir) lime leaves, thinly sliced
1 long red chilli, seeded and thinly sliced, for garnish

To soften the banana leaves and prevent them from splitting, put them in a hot oven for about 10–20 seconds, or blanch them briefly in boiling water. Cut the leaves into 12 circles 15 cm (6 in) in diameter with the fibre running lengthways.

Place one circle with the fibre running lengthways and another on top with the fibre running across. Make a 1 cm (½ in) deep tuck 4 cm (1½ in) long (4 cm in from the edge and no further) and pin securely with a small sharp toothpick. Repeat at the opposite point and at the two side points, making four tucks altogether. Flatten the base as best you can. Repeat to make six cups. Place a few basil leaves in the bottom of each cup and spoon in the fish filling until three-quarters full.

Fill a wok or a steamer pan with water, cover and bring to the boil over high heat. Place the banana cups on a plate. Use a plate that will fit on the rack of a traditional bamboo steamer basket or on a steamer rack inside the wok or pan. (If your wok or pan has a special steaming plate that will hold the cups flat, you may not need to put them on a separate plate.) Taking care not to burn your hands, set the rack or basket over the water and put the plate on the rack. Reduce the heat to a simmer, then cover and cook for 15–20 minutes. Check and replenish the water after 10 minutes.

When the cups are cooked the filling will puff and rise slightly. Turn off the heat and carefully transfer the cups to a serving plate. Spoon a little coconut cream on top and sprinkle with lime leaves and sliced chilli.

MAKES 6

Right: Use a bowl or plate as a guide when cutting the banana leaves into circles.

Far right: Form the banana leaves into six cups, securing them with sharp toothpicks.

Chapter 5

MEAT AND POULTRY

Barbecues, slow braises and deep-fried dishes using meat and poultry reflect the assimilation of many influences on Thai cuisine, from Southeast Asia, China, India and beyond.

KAI YAANG

Grilled Chicken

In Thailand, these whole grilled chickens are seen by the roadside rotating on open spits. Thai chickens are leaner than those found in Western countries but the taste will be similar. There are many flavouring variations used for grilled chickens.

MARINADE
4 coriander (cilantro) roots, finely chopped
4 garlic cloves, finely chopped
1 lemon grass stalk, white part only, finely chopped
3 tablespoons fish sauce
1/4 teaspoon ground white pepper
1 teaspoon palm sugar (jaggery)

1 chicken, spatchcocked
sweet chilli sauce (page 241), to serve
lime wedges, to serve

Using a pestle and mortar, pound the coriander roots, garlic, lemon grass, fish sauce, white pepper and palm sugar together, then spoon into a bowl. Add the chicken and rub the marinade all over the skin. Cover and marinate in the refrigerator for at least 3 hours, or overnight.

Heat a barbecue, char-grill or grill (broiler) until very hot. Cook the chicken for 20–30 minutes, turning it over at regular intervals.

Cut the chicken into pieces and serve with sweet chilli sauce and lime wedges.

SERVES 4

Muu Parlow

Braised Pork

1 large pork hock or 2 small ones
oil, for deep-frying
2 coriander (cilantro) roots, chopped
4 garlic cloves, crushed
2 teaspoons ground white pepper
4 slices of ginger
2 star anise

1 cinnamon stick
2 tablespoons palm sugar (jaggery)
2 tablespoons ketchap manis
2 tablespoons fish sauce
1.5 litres (52 fl oz/6 cups) chicken stock
4 hard-boiled eggs, shells removed

Put the pork hock in a saucepan of salted water and bring to the boil. Drain and repeat, then pat dry with paper towels. Heat a wok one-quarter filled with oil until very hot. Carefully add the pork hock to the wok and fry until brown. Loosely cover the wok with a lid if the oil spits. Remove the pork. Drain away all but 1 tablespoon of the oil.

Fry the coriander, garlic and pepper briefly, then add the ginger, star anise and cinnamon stick and fry for 1 minute. Add the sugar, ketchap manis, fish sauce and stock and bring to the boil. Add the pork and cook for 2 hours, or until the meat is falling off the bone. Add the eggs and cook for 10 minutes. Season with salt and serve with rice.

PICTURE ON OPPOSITE PAGE

SERVES 4

Neua Haeng

Dried Beef

coriander (cilantro) roots from 1 bunch, finely chopped
1 teaspoon cumin seeds, roasted
2 teaspoons coriander seeds, roasted
4 garlic cloves
1 teaspoon white peppercorns
2 tablespoons palm sugar (jaggery)

2 tablespoons soy sauce
350 g (12 oz) rump steak, thinly sliced
oil, for deep-frying
sticky rice (page 246), to serve
a chilli sauce, to serve

Using a pestle and mortar, pound the coriander roots, cumin seeds, coriander seeds, garlic cloves, white peppercorns and a pinch of salt into a paste. Add the palm sugar and soy sauce and mix until the sugar dissolves. Add the beef strips and mix well. Cover and marinate the beef strips in the refrigerator overnight.

Preheat the oven to its lowest setting. Take the beef strips out of the marinade and drape over wire cooling racks. Cook for 4 hours, or until dry and leathery. If the beef is not crisp, heat the oil in a wok and deep-fry the beef in batches until crisp. Drain on paper towels, then serve with sticky rice and chilli sauce.

SERVES 6

MUU PING

Pork on Sticks

Just like satay, pork on sticks is a popular snack as well as making an excellent party food and is ideal for informal occasions such as barbecues. It can be served with rice or sticky rice. No additional sauce is necessary with this recipe.

1 kg (2 lb 4 oz) fillet of pork
250 ml (9 fl oz/1 cup) coconut milk (page 245)
2 tablespoons coconut sugar
2 tablespoons light soy sauce
2 tablespoons oyster sauce
110 g (4 oz) Asian shallots, roughly chopped

4 garlic cloves, roughly chopped
5 coriander (cilantro) roots, finely chopped
2.5 cm (1 in) piece of ginger, sliced
1½ teaspoons ground turmeric
¼ teaspoon ground white pepper

Cut the fillet of pork into pieces 4 cm (1½ in) wide x 8 cm (3 in) long x 5 mm (¼ in) thick and put them in a bowl.

Mix the coconut milk, coconut sugar, light soy sauce, oyster sauce, shallots, garlic, coriander, ginger, turmeric and pepper in a bowl until the sugar has dissolved. Pour over the meat and mix using your fingers or a spoon. Cover with plastic wrap and refrigerate for at least 5 hours, or overnight, turning occasionally.

Soak 25 bamboo skewers, 18–20 cm (7–8 in) long, in water for 1 hour to help prevent them from burning during cooking.

Thread a piece of the marinated pork onto each skewer as if you were sewing a piece of material. If some pieces are small, thread two pieces onto each stick. Heat a barbecue or grill (broiler) to high heat. If using a grill, line the grill tray with a piece of foil.

Barbecue for 5–7 minutes on each side, or grill (broil) the pork for 10 minutes on each side, until cooked through and slightly charred. Turn frequently and brush the marinade sauce over the meat during cooking. If using the grill, cook a good distance below the heat. Serve hot or warm.

MAKES 25

The pork is threaded onto skewers using a sewing action.

Muu Yang

Barbecued Pork Spare Ribs

2–3 garlic cloves, chopped
1 tablespoon chopped coriander (cilantro) roots or
   ground coriander
6 tablespoons palm sugar (jaggery)
7 tablespoons plum sauce or tomato ketchup
2 tablespoons light soy sauce

2 tablespoons oyster sauce
1 teaspoon ground pepper
1/2 teaspoon ground star anise (optional)
900 g (2 lb) pork spare ribs, chopped into 13–15 cm
   (5–6 in) long pieces (baby back, if possible;
   ask your butcher to prepare it)

Using a pestle and mortar or a small blender, pound or blend the garlic and coriander roots into a paste. In a large bowl, combine all the ingredients and rub the marinade all over the ribs with your fingers. Cover with plastic wrap and marinate in the refrigerator for at least 3 hours, or overnight.

Preheat the oven to 180°C (350°F/Gas 4) or heat a barbecue. If cooking in the oven, place the ribs with all the marinade in a baking dish. Bake for 45–60 minutes, basting several times during cooking. If barbecuing, put the ribs on the grill, cover and cook for 45 minutes, turning and basting a couple of times. If the ribs do not go sufficiently brown after this time, grill (broil) them for 5 minutes on each side until they are well browned and slightly charred.

SERVES 4

Muu Thawt

Deep-fried Pork Spare Ribs

5 coriander (cilantro) roots, chopped
3 garlic cloves, finely chopped
1 tablespoon fish sauce
1 1/2 tablespoons oyster sauce
1/2 teaspoon ground white pepper

900 g (2 lb) pork spare ribs, chopped into 4–5 cm
   (1 1/2–2 in) long pieces (baby back, if possible;
   ask your butcher to prepare it)
vegetable oil, for deep-frying
sweet chilli sauce (page 241), to serve

Using a pestle and mortar or small blender, pound or blend the coriander roots and garlic into a paste. In a large bowl, combine the coriander paste, fish sauce, oyster sauce and ground white pepper. Using your fingertips, rub the marinade into the pork ribs, then cover and marinate in the refrigerator for at least 3 hours, or overnight.

Heat 6 cm (2 1/2 in) oil in a wok or deep frying pan over medium heat. When the oil seems hot, drop a small piece of garlic into it. If it sizzles immediately, the oil is ready. It is important not to have the oil too hot. Deep-fry half the spare ribs at a time for 15–20 minutes, or until golden brown. Drain on paper towels. Serve with sweet chilli sauce.

SERVES 4

Nok Gradtaa Thawt

Deep-fried Quail

Quail works well for dishes that would probably traditionally have used pigeon or turtle dove. Chicken pieces can also be used but the quails look more attractive on the plate. Serve alongside vegetable dishes or use as a starter.

5 white peppercorns
5 coriander seeds
¼ teaspoon cumin seeds
1 star anise
2 garlic cloves
2 tablespoons soy sauce

½ teaspoon palm sugar (jaggery)
4 quails
oil, for deep-frying
roast chilli sauce (page 240) or sweet chilli sauce
  (page 241), to serve

Using a pestle and mortar, pound together the peppercorns, coriander seeds, cumin seeds, star anise and a pinch of salt. Add the garlic, soy sauce and palm sugar and pound to a paste.

Rub the paste all over the quails, cover and marinate in the refrigerator for at least 3 hours.

Heat the oil in a wok or deep frying pan until a piece of bread dropped into the oil sizzles and turns brown. Pat the quails dry with paper towels.

Add the quails and fry them for about 10 minutes, turning them so that they cook on all sides. Make sure the oil gets inside the quails as well. Drain well and sprinkle with a little more salt.

Cut the quails into quarters and serve with roast chilli sauce or sweet chilli sauce.

PICTURE ON PAGE 120

SERVES 4

Right: Use your fingertips to rub the paste all over the quails.

Far right: Deep-fry the quails until golden brown, then remove from the oil with a slotted spoon.

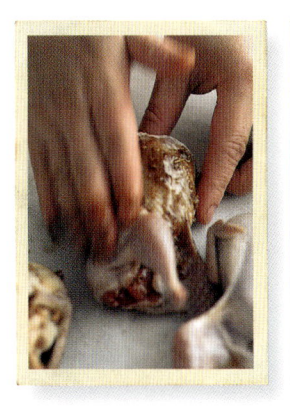

Deep-fried Quail (recipe on page 119)

MUU WAAN

Caramel Pork

Caramel pork has a relatively sweet flavour and is best served with steamed jasmine rice or sticky rice and a sharp-flavoured dish like green papaya salad or pomelo salad. It will keep for a few days in the refrigerator and can be made in advance.

vegetable oil, for deep-frying
75 g (3 oz) Asian shallots, thinly sliced
6 garlic cloves, finely chopped
500 g (1 lb 2 oz) shoulder or leg of pork,
   cut into thin slices

1 tablespoon oyster sauce
1 tablespoon light soy sauce
1 tablespoon fish sauce
4 tablespoons palm sugar (jaggery)
¼ teaspoon ground white pepper

Heat 5 cm (2 in) oil in a deep saucepan or wok over medium heat and deep-fry the shallots until they are golden brown. Be careful not to burn them. Remove them from the wok with a slotted spoon and drain on paper towels.

Drain the oil from the saucepan or wok, leaving 2 tablespoons in the pan. Stir-fry the garlic in the oil until light brown, add the pork and stir-fry for a few minutes. Add the oyster sauce, light soy sauce, fish sauce, sugar and ground pepper and continue cooking for about 5 minutes, or until all the liquid has evaporated and the mixture forms a thick sticky sauce.

Spoon onto a serving plate and sprinkle with the crisp shallots. Serve as required.

SERVES 4

Chapter 6

CURRIES

A glorious balance of spices and herbs is prerequisite when making a curry. And, while considerations of flavour are paramount, fragrance is an important factor, too.

Kaeng Phanaeng Neua

Panaeng Beef Curry

Panaeng curry is a dry, rich, thick curry made with small amounts of coconut milk and a dry curry paste, which has red chillies, lemon grass, galangal and peanuts. It is not too hot and has a sweet and sour taste. You can use any tender cut of beef.

2 tablespoons vegetable oil
2 tablespoons dry curry paste (page 237) or bought paste
700 g (1 lb 9 oz) beef flank steak, sliced into strips
185 ml (6 fl oz/¾ cup) coconut milk (page 245)
1 tablespoon fish sauce

1 tablespoon palm sugar (jaggery)
3 tablespoons tamarind purée
2 makrut (kaffir) lime leaves, thinly sliced, for garnish
½ long red chilli, seeded and thinly sliced, for garnish
cucumber relish (page 243), to serve

Heat the oil in a saucepan or wok and stir-fry the curry paste over medium heat for 2 minutes, or until fragrant.

Add the beef and stir for 5 minutes. Add nearly all of the coconut milk, the fish sauce, palm sugar and tamarind purée and reduce the heat to low. Simmer, uncovered, for 5–7 minutes. Although

this is meant to be a dry curry, you can add a little more water during cooking if it is drying out too much. Taste, then adjust the seasoning if necessary.

Spoon the curry into a serving bowl, spoon the last bit of coconut milk over the top and sprinkle with makrut lime leaves and chilli slices. Serve with cucumber relish.

SERVES 4

As with many Thai curries, this one cooks relatively quickly. Keep the meat moving around the wok until you add the liquid.

Kaeng Khiaw-Waan Kai

Green Curry with Chicken

This familiar classic, which should never be extremely hot, has as its base a paste of chillies, galangal and lemon grass. Bitter vegetables such as Thai eggplant offset the sweetness of the coconut cream. Tender steak can be used instead of chicken.

60 ml (2 fl oz/¼ cup) coconut cream (page 245)
2 tablespoons green curry paste (page 238)
  or bought paste
350 g (12 oz) boneless, skinless chicken thighs, sliced
440 ml (15 fl oz/1¾ cups) coconut milk (page 245)
2½ tablespoons fish sauce
1 tablespoon palm sugar (jaggery)

350 g (12 oz) mixed Thai eggplants (aubergines),
  cut into quarters, and pea eggplants (aubergines)
50 g (2 oz) galangal, julienned
7 makrut (kaffir) lime leaves, torn in half
a handful of Thai sweet basil leaves, for garnish
1 long red chilli, seeded and finely sliced, for garnish

Put the coconut cream in a wok or saucepan and simmer over medium heat for about 5 minutes, or until the cream separates and a layer of oil forms on the surface. Stir the cream if it starts to brown around the edges. Add the curry paste, stir well to combine and cook until fragrant.

Add the chicken and stir for a few minutes. Add nearly all of the coconut milk, the fish sauce and palm sugar and simmer over medium heat for another 5 minutes.

Add the eggplants and cook, stirring occasionally, for about 5 minutes or until the eggplants are cooked. Add the galangal and makrut lime leaves. Taste, then adjust the seasoning if necessary. Spoon into a serving bowl and sprinkle with the last bit of coconut milk, as well as the basil leaves and chilli slices.

SERVES 4

Various types of eggplant are used in Thailand and the bitter taste is very popular. They don't take long to cook.

KAENG PAA

Jungle Curry with Prawns

Jungle curry, a very hot curry, is common to the countryside, particularly in northern Thailand. It is traditionally made with local catfish but works well with any fish, or with prawns as in this recipe. It can be made with pork and most fresh vegetables.

JUNGLE CURRY PASTE
8 bird's eye chillies, chopped
2 cm (3/4 in) piece of galangal, chopped
2 lemon grass stalks, white part only, finely chopped
4 Asian shallots, finely chopped
4 garlic cloves, thinly sliced
1/2 teaspoon shrimp paste

400 g (14 oz) raw prawns (shrimp)
1 tablespoon oil
4 baby sweet corn, each cut into half lengthways
   on an angle

75 g (3 oz) Thai eggplants (aubergines), cut in halves
   or quarters
50 g (2 oz) pea eggplants (aubergines)
50 g (2 oz) straw or button mushrooms, halved if large
1 tablespoon fish sauce
1/2 teaspoon palm sugar (jaggery)
2–3 makrut (kaffir) lime leaves, torn into pieces,
   for garnish
a handful of holy basil or Thai sweet basil leaves,
   for garnish

Put all the jungle curry paste ingredients in a pestle and mortar and pound until smooth. Alternatively, put the ingredients in a small food processor with 2 tablespoons water and process to a smooth paste.

Peel and devein the prawns and cut each prawn along the back so it opens like a butterfly (leave each prawn joined along the base and at the tail).

Heat the oil in a wok or saucepan and stir-fry 2 tablespoons of the curry paste until fragrant. Add 410 ml (14 fl oz/1²/₃ cups) water and reduce the heat to medium. Add the sweet corn and eggplants and cook for 1–2 minutes. Add the mushrooms, prawns, fish sauce and sugar. Cook until the prawns open and turn pink. Taste, then adjust the seasoning if necessary. Sprinkle with the makrut lime leaves and basil leaves before serving.

SERVES 4

Far left: Stir-fry the curry paste to bring out the flavour.

Left: Once you have added all the ingredients, cook the curry until the prawns open and turn pink.

Kaeng Phanaeng Kung
Prawns with Thai Sweet Basil Leaves

The sauce for this dish should be thick, hot and sweet so make sure your wok is hot enough to reduce the coconut milk as it hits the surface.

600 g (1 lb 5 oz) raw prawns (shrimp)
2 tablespoons vegetable oil
2 tablespoons dry curry paste (page 237) or bought paste
185 ml (6 fl oz/^{3}/$_4$ cup) coconut milk (page 245)

2 teaspoons fish sauce
2 teaspoons palm sugar (jaggery)
a handful of Thai sweet basil leaves, for garnish
1 long red chilli, seeded and thinly sliced, for garnish

Peel and devein the prawns and cut each prawn along the back so it opens like a butterfly (leave each prawn joined along the base and at the tail, leaving the tail attached).

Heat the oil in a saucepan or wok and stir-fry the dry curry paste over medium heat for 2 minutes, or until fragrant.

Add the coconut milk, fish sauce and palm sugar and cook for a few seconds. Add the prawns and cook for a few minutes, or until the prawns are cooked through. Taste, then adjust the seasoning if necessary. Spoon into a serving bowl and garnish with basil leaves and chillies.

SERVES 4

Kaeng Hangleh Muu
Chiang Mai Pork Curry

500 g (1 lb 2 oz) pork belly, cut into cubes
2 tablespoons oil
2 garlic cloves, crushed
2 tablespoons Chiang Mai curry paste (page 237) or bought paste
4 Asian shallots, smashed with the blade of a cleaver

4 cm (1^1/$_2$ in) piece of ginger, shredded
4 tablespoons roasted unsalted peanuts
3 tablespoons tamarind purée
2 tablespoons fish sauce
2 tablespoons palm sugar (jaggery)

Blanch the pork in boiling water for 1 minute, then drain well.

Heat the oil in a wok or saucepan and fry the garlic for 1 minute. Add the curry paste and stir-fry until fragrant. Add the pork, shallots, ginger

and peanuts and stir briefly. Add the tamarind and 500 ml (17 fl oz/2 cups) water. Bring to the boil.

Add the fish sauce and sugar and simmer for about 1^1/$_2$ hours, or until the pork is very tender. Add more water as the pork cooks, if necessary.

SERVES 4

Kaeng Muu Phrik Thai Orn

Red Pork Curry with Green Peppercorns

Peppercorns add a distinctive, very fresh and spicy, not too hot, taste to this dish. You can use pork, as suggested, or thinly sliced chicken thighs. Cooked baby potatoes and bamboo shoots are a popular addition to this curry.

60 ml (2 fl oz/¼ cup) coconut cream (page 245)

2 tablespoons red curry paste (page 236) or bought paste

3 tablespoons fish sauce

1½ tablespoons palm sugar (jaggery)

500 g (1 lb 2 oz) lean pork, thinly sliced

440 ml (15 fl oz/1¾ cups) coconut milk (page 245)

280 g (10 oz) Thai eggplants (aubergines), cut in halves or quarters, or 1 eggplant (aubergine), cubed

75 g (3 oz) fresh green peppercorns, cleaned

7 makrut (kaffir) lime leaves, torn in half

2 long red chillies, seeded and thinly sliced, for garnish

Put the coconut cream in a wok or saucepan and simmer over medium heat for about 5 minutes, or until the cream separates and a layer of oil forms on the surface. Stir the cream if it starts to brown around the edges.

Add the curry paste, stir well to combine and cook until fragrant. Add the fish sauce and palm sugar and cook for 2 minutes, or until the mixture begins to darken. Add the pork and stir for 5–7 minutes.

Add the coconut milk to the saucepan or wok and simmer over medium heat for another 5 minutes. Add the eggplants and green peppercorns and cook for 5 minutes. Add the makrut lime leaves. Taste, then adjust the seasoning if necessary. Transfer to a serving bowl and sprinkle with the sliced chillies.

SERVES 4

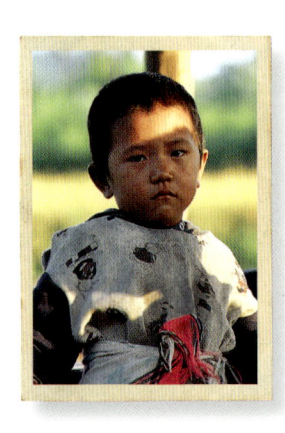 

Kaeng Kung Mangkawn

Spicy Lobster and Pineapple Curry

Even though this red curry is expensive because of the lobster, it is an excellent choice for special occasions. You can use large prawns or crab halves if you like. Also, you can make the sauce and serve it with barbecued lobster halves.

60 ml (2 fl oz/¼ cup) coconut cream (page 245)
2 tablespoons red curry paste (page 236) or
  bought paste
1 tablespoon fish sauce
1 tablespoon palm sugar (jaggery)
250 ml (9 fl oz/1 cup) coconut milk (page 245)
200 g (7 oz) fresh pineapple, cut into bite-sized wedges

300 g (11 oz) lobster tail meat
3 makrut (kaffir) lime leaves, 2 roughly torn and
  1 shredded
1 tablespoon tamarind purée
50 g (2 oz/1 cup) Thai sweet basil leaves, for garnish
1 large red chilli, thinly sliced, for garnish

Put the coconut cream in a wok or saucepan and simmer over medium heat for about 5 minutes, or until the cream separates and a layer of oil forms on the surface. Stir the cream if it starts to brown around the edges.

Add the curry paste, stir well to combine and cook until fragrant. Add the fish sauce and sugar and stir to combine. Cook for 4–5 minutes, stirring constantly. The mixture should darken.

Stir in the coconut milk and the pineapple and simmer for 6–8 minutes to soften the pineapple. Add the lobster tail meat, makrut lime leaves, tamarind purée and basil leaves. Cook for another 5–6 minutes, or until the lobster is firm. Serve with basil leaves and sliced chilli on top.

SERVES 4

Kaeng Khiaw-Waan Luuk Chin Pla

Green Curry with Fish Balls

This is a classic dish using fish balls or dumplings rather than pieces of fish but, if time is short, slices of fish are acceptable. The fish is processed, then pounded, to give it more texture. Serve with salted eggs (page 247), and rice.

350 g (12 oz) white fish fillets, without skin and bone, roughly cut into pieces
60 ml (2 fl oz/¼ cup) coconut cream (page 245)
2 tablespoons green curry paste (page 238) or bought paste
440 ml (15 fl oz/1¾ cups) coconut milk (page 245)
350 g (12 oz) mixed Thai eggplants (aubergines), quartered, and pea eggplants (aubergines)

2 tablespoons fish sauce
2 tablespoons palm sugar (jaggery)
50 g (2 oz) galangal, thinly sliced
3 makrut (kaffir) lime leaves, torn in half
a handful of holy basil leaves, for garnish
½ long red chilli, seeded and thinly sliced, for garnish

In a food processor or blender, chop the fish into a smooth paste. (If you have a pestle and mortar, pound the fish paste for another 10 minutes to give it a chewy texture.)

Put the coconut cream in a wok or saucepan and simmer over medium heat for about 5 minutes, or until the coconut cream separates and a layer of oil forms on the surface. Stir the cream if it starts to brown around the edges. Add the curry paste, stir well to combine and cook until fragrant. Add nearly all of the coconut milk and mix well.

Use a spoon or your wet hands to shape the fish paste into small balls or discs, about 2 cm (¾ in) across, and drop them into the coconut milk. Add the eggplants, fish sauce and sugar and cook for 12–15 minutes, stirring occasionally, until the fish and eggplants are cooked.

Stir in the galangal and makrut lime leaves. Taste, then adjust the seasoning if necessary. Spoon into a serving bowl and sprinkle with the last bit of coconut milk, basil leaves and sliced chilli.

SERVES 4

Far left: Use wet hands to roll the fish mixture into balls.

Left: Drop all the fish balls into the curry at the same time so they cook evenly.

Food Journey

FLAVOURINGS

Thai cuisine is built on a large number of highly flavoured aromatic ingredients. These are used, despite their diversity, to produce an overall effect of some sophistication, balance and subtlety.

Though curry pastes often include dry spices, the majority of Thai seasonings are fresh and pungent. These define the flavour that is 'Thai', as well as being responsible for adding texture to dishes. Thai flavourings are combined to give as harmonious an effect as possible, the balance of hot, sour, sweet and salty being paramount.

Hot (phed), in nearly all cases, comes from chillies, though it is sometimes supplemented with fresh green peppercorns or black or white pepper. There are about a dozen chillies used in Thai cuisine, each type with a different aroma, flavour and degree of heat. Chillies are used fresh or dried, depending on the recipe. Sour (priaw) comes from lime juice, the zest and leaves of makrut (kaffir) limes, tamarind, and to a lesser extent, ambarella (a Southeast Asian fruit like a small mango). Sour can also come from coconut vinegar or pickles. Sweet (waan) is imparted by the use of palm sugar (jaggery), coconut sugar, cane sugar and coconut milk. Salt (khem) comes from fish sauce and shrimp paste. Salt itself is used as an ingredient but never as a condiment, except when sprinkled on fresh fruit.

Also important in Thai cuisine is fragrance. The aroma of various herbs, vegetables, rhizomes and leaves add a unique quality to Thai dishes. Robust herbs and roots such as lemon grass, ginger, galangal, turmeric, Chinese keys and coriander (cilantro) roots are used to make pastes and can be cooked for a reasonable length of time. Garlic and shallots are also important and they are often simply smashed with the blade of a cleaver rather then being peeled and finely chopped. Leaf herbs such as coriander (cilantro), Thai sweet basil, lemon and holy basil, and common mint occur frequently. Less well known herbs include long-leaf coriander. These are at their most aromatic when eaten raw, or cooked for the bare minimum of time. Sprigs of fresh herbs such as mint (sa-ra-nae) and Thai sweet basil (bai horapha) are also eaten alongside some dishes. Fragrant pandanus leaves are used as a wrapping and as a flavouring. They are said to have a vanilla flavour, and green pandanus essence is used much like vanilla essence in many sweets.

KAENG PHET PET YAANG

Red Curry with Roasted Duck and Lychees

In Thailand, this speciality dish is often served during the traditional family feasting that accompanies celebrations including the ordination of Buddhist monks, weddings and New Year. This is very rich, so serve it alongside a salad to cut through the sauce.

60 ml (2 fl oz/¼ cup) coconut cream (page 245)
2 tablespoons red curry paste (page 236) or
  bought paste
½ roasted duck, boned and chopped
440 ml (15 fl oz/1¾ cups) coconut milk (page 245)
2 tablespoons fish sauce

1 tablespoon palm sugar (jaggery)
225 g (8 oz) tin lychees, drained
110 g (4 oz) baby tomatoes
7 makrut (kaffir) lime leaves, torn in half
a handful of Thai sweet basil leaves, for garnish
1 long red chilli, seeded and thinly sliced, for garnish

Put the coconut cream in a wok or saucepan and simmer over medium heat for about 5 minutes, or until the cream separates and a layer of oil forms on the surface. Stir the cream if it starts to brown around the edges. Add the curry paste, stir well to combine and cook until fragrant.

Add the roasted duck and stir for 5 minutes. Add the coconut milk, fish sauce and palm sugar and simmer over medium heat for another 5 minutes.

Add the lychees and baby tomatoes and cook for 1–2 minutes. Add the makrut lime leaves. Taste, then adjust the seasoning if necessary. Spoon into a serving bowl and sprinkle with the basil leaves and sliced chilli.

SERVES 4

This curry, with its combination of coconut milk, duck and fruit, is very rich. Cook the lychees for only a few minutes.

KAENG PLAA KUP KLUAY LAI MAMUANG
Snapper with Green Banana and Mango

Green banana is very starchy, much more like a vegetable than a fruit. Here it is used in a yellow curry alongside another fruit, green mango, which acts as a souring agent. Raw vegetables are often served as an accompaniment to counteract the chilli heat.

1 teaspoon salt
1 teaspoon ground turmeric
1 small green banana or plantain, thinly sliced
60 ml (2 fl oz/¼ cup) coconut cream (page 245)
2 tablespoons yellow curry paste (page 238) or
   bought paste
1 tablespoon fish sauce

1 teaspoon palm sugar (jaggery)
400 g (14 oz) snapper or other white fish fillets, cut into
   large cubes
315 ml (11 fl oz/1¼ cups) coconut milk (page 245)
1 small green mango, cut into thin slices
1 large green chilli, thinly sliced
12 Thai sweet basil leaves

Bring a small saucepan of water to the boil. Add the salt, turmeric and banana slices and simmer for 10 minutes, then drain.

Put the coconut cream in a wok or a saucepan and simmer over medium heat for about 5 minutes, or until the coconut cream separates and a layer of oil forms on the surface. Stir the cream if it starts to brown around the edges. Add the curry paste, stir well to combine and cook until fragrant. Add the fish sauce and sugar and cook for 2 minutes, or until the mixture begins to darken.

Add the fish pieces and stir well to coat the fish in the curry mixture. Slowly add the coconut milk until it has all been incorporated.

Add the banana, mango, green chilli and most of the basil leaves to the pan and gently stir to combine all the ingredients, cooking for a minute or two. Garnish with the remaining basil.

SERVES 4

The banana and green mango are only cooked for a short time.

Kaeng Matsaman Neua

Massaman Curry with Beef

This curry has many characteristics of southern Thai cooking. The sweet flavours and spices dominate, even though the curry is moderately hot. It also has a sour taste from the tamarind. This dish is one of the few Thai dishes with potatoes and peanuts.

2 pieces of cinnamon stick

10 cardamom seeds

5 cloves

2 tablespoons vegetable oil

2 tablespoons massaman curry paste (page 236) or bought paste

800 g (1 lb 12 oz) beef flank or rump steak, cut into 5 cm (2 in) cubes

410 ml (14 fl oz/1²/₃ cups) coconut milk (page 245)

250 ml (9 fl oz/1 cup) beef stock

2–3 potatoes, cut into 2.5 cm (1 in) pieces

2 cm (³/₄ in) piece of ginger, shredded

3 tablespoons fish sauce

3 tablespoons palm sugar (jaggery)

110 g (4 oz/²/₃ cup) roasted salted peanuts, without skin

3 tablespoons tamarind purée

Dry-fry the cinnamon stick, cardamom seeds and cloves in a saucepan or wok over low heat. Stir all the ingredients around for 2–3 minutes, or until fragrant. Remove from the pan.

Heat the oil in the same saucepan or wok. Stir-fry the curry paste over medium heat for 2 minutes, or until fragrant. Add the beef to the pan and stir for 5 minutes.

Add the coconut milk, stock, potatoes, ginger, fish sauce, palm sugar, three-quarters of the roasted peanuts, tamarind purée and the dry-fried spices. Reduce the heat to low and gently simmer for 50– 60 minutes, or until the meat is tender and the potatoes are just cooked. Taste, then adjust the seasoning if necessary. Spoon into a serving bowl and garnish with the rest of the roasted peanuts.

SERVES 4

Kaeng Karii Kai

Yellow Chicken Curry with Peppercorns

Fresh peppercorns have a fragrant, pungent quality that lifts the flavour of any curry in which they are used. You should beware of eating a whole sprig in one go though because, just like the pepper they become, they are extremely hot.

60 ml (2 fl oz/¼ cup) coconut cream (page 245)

2 tablespoons yellow curry paste (page 238) or bought paste

1 tablespoon fish sauce

2 teaspoons palm sugar (jaggery)

¼ teaspoon turmeric

600 g (1 lb 5 oz) boneless, skinless chicken thighs, cut into thin slices

440 ml (15 fl oz/1¾ cups) coconut milk (page 245)

100 g (3 oz) bamboo shoots, thinly sliced

4 sprigs fresh green peppercorns

4–6 makrut (kaffir) lime leaves

12 Thai sweet basil leaves

Put the coconut cream in a wok or saucepan and simmer over medium heat for about 5 minutes, or until the cream separates and a layer of oil forms on the surface. Stir the cream if it starts to brown around the edges.

Add the curry paste, stir well to combine and cook until fragrant. Add the fish sauce, palm sugar and turmeric and stir well. Cook for 2–3 minutes, stirring occasionally, until the mixture darkens.

Add the chicken to the pan and stir to coat all the pieces evenly in the spice mixture. Cook over medium heat for 5 minutes, stirring occasionally and adding the coconut milk 1 tablespoon at a time. Add the bamboo shoots, peppercorns, lime and basil leaves and cook for another 5 minutes.

SERVES 4

Chapter 7

STIR-FRIES

Loved the world over for their speed and versatility, the technique
of stir-frying in Thailand is underpinned by the layering of textures
and can be delicate or robust in flavour.

Phat Thaleh

Mixed Seafood with Chillies

The bird's eye chillies give this dish quite a lot of heat but if you would like it even hotter, just add a few more. Serve with plenty of jasmine rice and a coconut-based curry to help take some of the sting out of the dish.

450 g (1 lb) mixed fresh seafood such as prawns (shrimp), squid tubes, small scallops
2 tablespoons vegetable oil
3–4 garlic cloves, finely chopped
1 green capsicum (pepper), cut into bite-sized pieces
1 small onion, cut into thin slices
5 snake (yard-long) beans, cut into 2.5 cm (1 in) pieces
1 cm (1/2 in) piece of ginger, finely grated

4 bird's eye chillies, lightly bruised
1 tablespoon oyster sauce
1/2 tablespoon light soy sauce
1/4 teaspoon sugar
1 long red chilli (optional), seeded and sliced diagonally
1–2 spring onions (scallions), thinly sliced
a few holy basil leaves, or coriander (cilantro) leaves, for garnish

Peel and devein the prawns and cut each prawn open along the back so it opens like a butterfly (leave each prawn joined along the base and at the tail). Peel off the outer skin of the squid and rinse out the insides of the tubes. Cut each in half and open out the pieces. Score the inside of each squid with diagonal cuts to make a diamond pattern, then cut them into squares. Carefully slice off and discard any vein, membrane or hard white muscle from each scallop. Scallops can be left whole, or, if large, cut each in half.

Heat the oil in a wok or frying pan and stir-fry the garlic over medium heat until light brown.

Add the capsicum, onion, beans, ginger and chillies and stir-fry for 1 minute.

Add the seafood to the wok in stages, prawns first, then scallops, adding the squid last and tossing after each addition. Add the oyster sauce, light soy sauce and sugar and stir-fry for 2–3 minutes, or until the prawns open and turn pink and all the seafood is cooked.

Add the chilli and spring onions and toss together. Taste, then adjust the seasoning if necessary. Spoon onto a serving plate and sprinkle with basil or coriander leaves.

SERVES 4

HET PHAT TAO-HUU

Mushrooms with Tofu

Tofu and mushrooms are commonly used together in Chinese dishes, just as they are here in this Thai dish. The blandness of the tofu is a contrast to both the texture and flavour of the mushrooms. For the best flavour, use the type of mushrooms suggested.

350 g (12 oz) firm tofu (bean curd)
1 teaspoon sesame oil
2 teaspoons light soy sauce
1/4 teaspoon ground black pepper, plus some to sprinkle
1 tablespoon finely shredded ginger
100 ml (4 fl oz) vegetable stock or water
2 tablespoons light soy sauce
2 teaspoons cornflour (cornstarch)

1/2 teaspoon sugar
11/2 tablespoons vegetable oil
2 garlic cloves, finely chopped
200 g (7 oz) oyster mushrooms, hard stalks removed, cut in half if large
200 g (7 oz) shiitake mushrooms, hard stalks removed
2 spring onions (scallions), sliced diagonally, for garnish
1 long red chilli, seeded and thinly sliced, for garnish

Drain each block of tofu and cut into 2.5 cm (1 in) pieces. Put them in a shallow dish and sprinkle with the sesame oil, light soy sauce, ground pepper and ginger. Leave to marinate for 30 minutes.

Mix the stock with the light soy sauce, cornflour and sugar in a small bowl until smooth.

Heat the oil in a wok or frying pan and stir-fry the garlic over medium heat until light brown. Add all the mushrooms to the wok and stir-fry for 3–4 minutes, or until the mushrooms are cooked. Add the cornflour liquid, then carefully add the tofu and gently mix for 1–2 minutes. Taste, then adjust the seasoning if necessary.

Spoon onto a serving plate and sprinkle with spring onions, chilli slices and ground pepper.

SERVES 2

Stir-fry all of the mushrooms together before adding the sauce and the tofu.

KAI PHAT BAI KA-PHRAO

Chicken with Crispy Holy Basil Leaves

This is one of the most common dishes you will come across in Thailand. Holy basil comes in two colours, red and green. It has a hot, slightly sharp flavour and is often used in conjunction with chillies in stir-fries. Serve with plenty of rice.

500 g (1 lb 2 oz) boneless, skinless chicken breast, thinly sliced
4–5 garlic cloves, finely chopped
4–5 small red or green bird's eye chillies, lightly crushed
1 tablespoon fish sauce
2 tablespoons oyster sauce

vegetable oil, for deep-frying
2 handfuls of holy basil leaves
2 tablespoons vegetable or chicken stock, or water
½ teaspoon sugar
1 red capsicum (pepper), cut into bite-sized pieces
1 medium onion, cut into thin wedges

Mix the chicken slices, garlic, chillies, fish sauce and oyster sauce in a bowl. Cover with plastic wrap and marinate in the refrigerator for at least 30 minutes.

Heat 5 cm (2 in) oil in a wok or deep frying pan over medium heat. When the oil seems hot, drop a few basil leaves into it. If they sizzle immediately, the oil is ready. Deep-fry three-quarters of the basil leaves for 1 minute, or until they are all crisp. Lift out with a slotted spoon and drain on paper towels. Discard the remaining oil.

Heat 2 tablespoons oil in the same wok or frying pan and stir-fry half the chicken over high heat for 3–4 minutes. Remove from the pan and repeat with the remaining chicken. Return all the chicken to the wok.

Add the stock and sugar to the wok, then add the capsicum and onion, and stir-fry for 1–2 minutes. Stir in the fresh basil leaves. Taste, then adjust the seasoning if necessary. Garnish with the crispy basil leaves.

SERVES 4

Neua Phat Bai Hohrapha
Beef with Thai Sweet Basil Leaves

1 tablespoon fish sauce
3 tablespoons oyster sauce
4 tablespoons vegetable or chicken stock, or water
1/2 teaspoon sugar
2 tablespoons vegetable oil
4 garlic cloves, finely chopped

3 bird's eye chillies, lightly crushed with the side of
   a cleaver
500 g (1 lb 2 oz) tender rump or fillet steak, thinly sliced
1 medium onion, cut into thin wedges
2 handfuls of Thai sweet basil leaves

Mix the fish sauce, oyster sauce, stock and sugar in a small bowl.

Heat the oil in a wok or frying pan and stir-fry half the garlic over medium heat until light brown. Add half the crushed chillies and half the meat and stir-fry over high heat for 2–3 minutes, or until the meat is cooked. Remove from the wok and repeat with the remaining garlic, chillies and meat. Return all the meat to the wok.

Add the onion and the fish sauce mixture and stir-fry for another minute. Add the basil leaves and stir-fry until the basil begins to wilt. Taste, then adjust the seasoning if necessary. Spoon onto a serving plate.

SERVES 4

Kai Phat Nam Phrik Phao
Chicken with Chilli Jam

2 teaspoons fish sauce
2 tablespoons oyster sauce
60 ml (2 fl oz/1/4 cup) coconut milk (page 245)
1/2 teaspoon sugar
2 1/2 tablespoons vegetable oil
6 garlic cloves, finely chopped

1–1 1/2 tablespoons chilli jam (page 240), to taste
500 g (1 lb 2 oz) boneless, skinless chicken breast,
   thinly sliced
a handful of holy basil leaves
1 long red or green chilli, seeded and thinly sliced,
   for garnish

Mix the fish sauce, oyster sauce, coconut milk and sugar in a small bowl.

Heat the oil in a wok or frying pan and stir-fry half the garlic over medium heat until light brown. Add half the chilli jam and stir-fry for 2 minutes, or until fragrant. Add half the chicken and stir-fry over high heat for 2–3 minutes. Remove from the wok. Repeat with the remaining garlic, chilli jam and chicken. Return all the chicken to the wok. Add the fish sauce mixture and stir-fry for a few seconds, or until the chicken is cooked. Taste, then adjust the seasoning if necessary. Stir in the basil leaves. Garnish with chilli slices.

SERVES 4

THUA PHAT MUU
Pork with Snake Beans

1 tablespoon oyster sauce
1 tablespoon light soy sauce
¼ teaspoon sugar
2 tablespoons vegetable oil
4 garlic cloves, finely chopped

350 g (12 oz) pork fillet, thinly sliced
250 g (9 oz) snake (yard-long) beans, cut into 5 cm
   (2 in) pieces
½ long red chilli, seeded, shredded, for garnish (optional)

Mix the oyster sauce, light soy sauce, sugar and 2 tablespoons water in a small bowl.

Heat the oil in a wok or frying pan and stir-fry the garlic over medium heat until light brown. Add the pork and stir-fry over high heat for

3–5 minutes, or until the pork is cooked. Add the beans and sauce mixture and stir-fry for 4 minutes. Taste, then adjust the seasoning if necessary.

Transfer to a serving plate and garnish with the chilli slices.

PICTURE ON PAGE 164

SERVES 4

PHAT NEUA TAO JIAW DAM
Beef with Black Bean Sauce

1 tablespoon black beans, rinsed and roughly mashed
3 tablespoons vegetable or chicken stock, or water
1 tablespoon fish sauce
1 tablespoon oyster sauce
1 tablespoon sesame oil
½ teaspoon sugar
1 tablespoon vegetable oil

3–4 garlic cloves, finely chopped
250 g (9 oz) tender rump or fillet steak, thinly sliced
½ carrot, cut into fine matchsticks
4 snake (yard-long) beans, cut into 5 cm (2 in) lengths
2 spring onions (scallions), cut into 2.5 cm (1 in) lengths
a few coriander (cilantro) leaves, for garnish

Mix the black beans, stock, fish sauce, oyster sauce, sesame oil and sugar in a small bowl.

Heat the oil in a wok or frying pan. Stir-fry half of the garlic over medium heat until light brown. Add half the meat and stir-fry for 3–4 minutes, or until cooked. Remove from the wok. Repeat with the remaining garlic and meat. Return all the garlic and meat to the wok.

Add the carrot, beans and the sauce mixture to the wok and stir-fry for another 1–2 minutes. Taste, then adjust the seasoning if necessary. Stir in the spring onions and cook for a few seconds. Spoon onto a serving plate and garnish with coriander leaves.

SERVES 4

Pork with Snake Beans (recipe on page 163)

MUU PHAT KHING

Pork with Ginger

A hybrid dish, Chinese in style with the addition of fish sauce for a Thai flavour, this recipe is best made with firm, young, tender ginger with translucent skin. The aroma of the whole dish should be distinctly gingery as it arrives at the table.

15 g (½ oz) dried black fungus (about half a handful)
1 tablespoon fish sauce
1½ tablespoons oyster sauce
4 tablespoons vegetable or chicken stock, or water
½ teaspoon sugar
2 tablespoons vegetable oil
3–4 garlic cloves, finely chopped

500 g (1 lb 2 oz) lean pork, thinly sliced
25 g (1 oz) ginger, julienned
1 small onion, cut into 8 wedges
2 spring onions (scallions), diagonally sliced
ground white pepper, for sprinkling
1 long red chilli, seeded and finely sliced, for garnish
a few coriander (cilantro) leaves, for garnish

Soak the dried black fungus in a bowl of hot water for 2–3 minutes, or until soft, then drain.

Mix the fish sauce, oyster sauce, stock and sugar in a small bowl.

Heat the oil in a wok or frying pan and stir-fry half the garlic over medium heat until light brown. Add half the pork and stir-fry over high heat for 2–3 minutes, or until the pork is cooked. Remove from the wok. Repeat with the remaining garlic and pork. Return all the pork to the wok.

Add the ginger, onion, black fungus and the sauce mixture to the wok. Stir fry for 1–2 minutes. Taste, then adjust the seasoning if necessary. Stir in the spring onions.

Spoon onto a serving plate and sprinkle with ground pepper, chilli slices and coriander leaves.

SERVES 4

KAI PHAT MET MUANG HIMAPHAAN
Chicken with Cashew Nuts

This popular dish is typically Chinese but appears on many Thai restaurant menus. The cashews are actually a Thai addition. Frying the cashew nuts separately brings out their flavour and adds a more 'nutty' taste to the dish.

1–2 dried long red chillies
1 tablespoon fish sauce
2 tablespoons oyster sauce
3 tablespoons chicken or vegetable stock, or water
1/2–1 teaspoon sugar
4 tablespoons vegetable oil
80 g (3 oz/1/2 cup) cashew nuts
4–5 garlic cloves, finely chopped

500 g (1 lb 2 oz) boneless, skinless chicken breast, thinly sliced
1/2 red capsicum (pepper), cut into thin strips
1/2 carrot, sliced diagonally
1 small onion, cut into 6 wedges
2 spring onions (scallions), cut into 1 cm (1/2 in) lengths
ground white pepper, to sprinkle

Take the stems off the dried chillies, cut each chilli into 1 cm (1/2 in) pieces with scissors or a sharp knife and discard the seeds.

Mix the fish sauce, oyster sauce, stock and sugar in a small bowl.

Heat the oil in a wok over medium heat and stir-fry the cashew nuts for 2–3 minutes, or until light brown. Remove with a slotted spoon and drain on paper towels.

Stir-fry the chillies in the same oil over medium heat for 1 minute. They should darken but not blacken and burn. Remove with a slotted spoon.

Reheat the oil and stir-fry half the chopped garlic over medium heat until light brown. Add half the chicken and stir-fry over high heat for 4–5 minutes, or until the chicken is cooked. Remove from the wok and repeat with the remaining garlic and chicken. Return all the chicken to the wok.

Add the capsicum, carrot, onion and the sauce mixture to the wok and stir-fry for 1–2 minutes. Taste, then adjust the seasoning if necessary.

Add the cashew nuts, chillies and spring onions and toss well. Sprinkle with ground pepper.

SERVES 4

Muu Phat Priaw Waan

Pork with Sweet and Sour Sauce

Pork is the meat preferred in many areas of Thailand. This is a Thai version of the better known Chinese sweet and sour pork. The vegetables can be varied according to what is available, but choose ones that will still be crunchy when cooked.

225 g (8 oz) tin pineapple slices in light syrup, each slice cut into 4 pieces (reserve the syrup)
1½ tablespoons plum sauce (page 242) or tomato ketchup
2½ teaspoons fish sauce
1 tablespoon sugar
2 tablespoons vegetable oil
250 g (9 oz) pork, sliced

4 garlic cloves, finely chopped
¼ carrot, sliced
1 medium onion, cut into 8 slices
½ red capsicum (pepper), cut into bite-sized pieces
1 small cucumber, unpeeled, halved lengthways and cut into thick slices
1 tomato, cut into 4 slices, or 4–5 baby tomatoes
a few coriander (cilantro) leaves, for garnish

Mix all the pineapple syrup (about 6 tablespoons) with the plum sauce, fish sauce and sugar in a small bowl until smooth.

Heat the oil in a wok or deep frying pan over medium heat and fry the pork until browned and cooked. Lift out with a slotted spoon and drain on paper towels.

Add the garlic to the wok or pan and fry over medium heat for 1 minute, or until lightly browned. Add the carrot, onion and capsicum and stir-fry for 1–2 minutes. Add the cucumber, tomato, pineapple and the sauce and stir together for another minute. Taste, then adjust the seasoning if necessary.

Return the pork to the pan and gently stir. Spoon onto a plate and garnish with coriander leaves.

SERVES 4

Kung Phat Kra-Tiam

Stir-fried Garlic Prawns

Tiger prawns are extensively farmed in Thailand and appear in many dishes. You can, however, use different types of prawns depending on availability. This recipe has quite a lot of garlic so choose nice fresh, sweet bulbs to make the best of the flavour.

500 g (1 lb 2 oz) large raw prawns (shrimp)
18–20 coriander (cilantro) roots, roughly chopped
4–5 garlic cloves, roughly chopped
10 black peppercorns
1 tablespoon light soy sauce

1½ tablespoons oyster sauce
½ teaspoon sugar
3 tablespoons vegetable oil
a few coriander (cilantro) leaves, for garnish
1 long red chilli, seeded and thinly sliced, for garnish

Peel and devein the prawns and cut each prawn along the back so it opens like a butterfly (leave each prawn joined along the base and at the tail).

Using a pestle and mortar or a small blender, pound or grind the coriander roots and garlic into a rough paste. Add the peppercorns and continue to grind roughly.

Mix the light soy sauce, oyster sauce and sugar in a small bowl.

Heat the oil in a wok or frying pan and stir-fry the coriander paste for 1–2 minutes, or until the garlic starts to turn light brown and fragrant. Add the prawns and light soy sauce mixture and stir-fry for another 2–3 minutes, or until the prawns open and turn pink. Taste, then adjust the seasoning if necessary. Sprinkle with the coriander leaves and chilli slices.

SERVES 4

Muu Phat Kra-Tiam Phrik Thai
Pork with Garlic and Pepper

A classic combination of garlic and pepper is found in this Chinese-style dish. Thai garlic is less pungent than many other types of garlic. Crush the peppercorns just before you use them. Serve with a vegetable dish and jasmine rice.

1½ teaspoons black peppercorns
1 whole bulb of garlic, cloves roughly chopped
8–10 coriander (cilantro) roots, roughly chopped
3 tablespoons vegetable oil
500 g (1 lb 2 oz) pork fillet, cut into 5 cm (2 in) squares

1 tablespoon fish sauce
1 tablespoon light soy sauce
½ teaspoon sugar
garlic and chilli sauce (page 241), to serve

Using a pestle and mortar or a small blender, pound or blend the black peppercorns (just roughly) and spoon them into a small bowl.

Pound or blend the garlic and coriander roots into a paste and mix with the peppercorns.

Heat the oil in a wok or frying pan and stir-fry half the garlic and peppercorn paste over medium heat for 1–2 minutes, or until the garlic turns light brown and is fragrant. Add half the pork and stir-fry over high heat for 1 minute, then reduce the heat and cook for 2–3 minutes, or until the meat is cooked. Remove from the wok. Repeat with the remaining paste and pork. Return all the pork to the wok.

Add the fish sauce, light soy sauce and sugar to the wok. Stir-fry for 5 minutes, or until the pork starts to turn brown. Serve with garlic and chilli sauce.

SERVES 4

A granite pestle and mortar helps in many Thai recipes. A deep mortar is best when you have a lot of ingredients.

Chapter 8

NOODLES AND RICE

Egg, rice and mung bean noodles are popular in sustaining soups, while rice, including sticky rice, is the central part of a meal, featuring in everything from soups to desserts.

KUAYTIAW PHAT THAI
Thai Fried Noodles with Prawns

This is one of the most famous dishes in Thailand. Everyone who visits should try it, otherwise they have not really been there at all. To make it, you need to use small white noodles of the dried sen lek variety. You can substitute meat for prawns.

150 g (6 oz) dried noodles (sen lek)
300 g (11 oz) raw large prawns (shrimp)
3 tablespoons tamarind purée
2½ tablespoons fish sauce
2 tablespoons palm sugar (jaggery)
3 tablespoons vegetable oil
3–4 garlic cloves, finely chopped
2 eggs
85 g (3 oz) Chinese chives (1 bunch)

¼ teaspoon chilli powder, depending on taste
2 tablespoons dried shrimp, ground or pounded
2 tablespoons preserved turnip, finely chopped
2½–3 tablespoons chopped roasted peanuts
180 g (7 oz/2 cups) bean sprouts
3 spring onions (scallions), slivered
1 long red chilli, seeded and shredded, for garnish
a few coriander (cilantro) leaves, for garnish
lime wedges, to serve

Soak the noodles in hot water for 1–2 minutes, or until soft, then drain.

Peel and devein the prawns and cut each prawn along the back so it opens like a butterfly (leave each prawn joined along the base and at the tail, leaving the tail attached).

Combine the tamarind purée with the fish sauce and palm sugar in a bowl.

Heat 1½ tablespoons oil in a wok or frying pan and stir-fry the garlic over medium heat until it is light brown. Add the peeled prawns and cook for 2 minutes.

Using a spatula, move the prawns out from the middle of the wok. Add another 1½ tablespoons oil to the wok. Add the eggs and stir to scramble for 1 minute. Add the noodles and chives and stir-fry for a few seconds. Add the fish sauce mixture, chilli powder, dried shrimp, preserved turnip and half of the peanuts. Add half of the bean sprouts and spring onions. Test the noodles for tenderness and adjust the seasoning if necessary.

Spoon onto the serving plate and sprinkle with the remaining peanuts. Garnish with shredded chillies and coriander leaves. Place the lime wedges and remaining bean sprouts and spring onions at the side of the dish.

SERVES 4

KHAO PHAT SAPPAROT

Fried Rice with Pineapple

Fried rice originated in China and is now a staple snack in Thailand. It is not eaten instead of steamed rice but on its own. This is a unique way of presenting fried rice. It is a splendid dish to serve when pineapples are in season and easy to find.

1 fresh pineapple, leaves attached
2 tablespoons vegetable oil
1 egg, beaten with a pinch of salt
2–3 garlic cloves, finely chopped
150 g (6 oz) raw prawns (shrimp), peeled and deveined
150 g (6 oz) ham, finely chopped
25 g (1 oz) sweet corn kernels
25 g (1 oz) peas

1/2 red capsicum (pepper), finely diced
1 tablespoon thinly sliced ginger (optional)
280 g (10 oz/1 1/2 cups) cooked jasmine rice, refrigerated overnight
1 tablespoon light soy sauce
25 g (1 oz) roasted salted cashew nuts, roughly chopped
1 long red chilli, seeded and thinly sliced, for garnish
a few coriander (cilantro) leaves, for garnish

Preheat the oven to 180°C (350°F/Gas 4). Cut the pineapple in half, lengthways. Scoop the flesh out of both halves using a tablespoon and a paring knife, to leave two shells with a 1 cm (1/2 in) border of flesh attached. Cut the flesh into small cubes. Put half the cubes in a bowl and refrigerate the rest for eating later.

Wrap the pineapple leaves in foil to prevent them from burning. Place the shells on a baking tray and bake for 10–15 minutes. This will seal in the juice and prevent it leaking into the fried rice when it is placed in the shells.

Heat 1 tablespoon oil in a wok or frying pan over medium heat. Pour in the egg and swirl the pan so that the egg coats it, forming a thin omelette. Cook for 2 minutes, or until the egg is set and

slightly brown on the underside, then flip over to brown the other side. Remove from the pan and allow to cool slightly. Roll up and cut into strips.

Heat 1 tablespoon oil in the wok or frying pan and stir-fry the garlic over medium heat until light brown. Add the prawns, ham, sweet corn, peas, capsicum and ginger. Stir-fry for 2 minutes, or until the prawns open and turn pink. Add the cooked rice, light soy sauce and the bowl of fresh pineapple and toss together over medium heat for 5–7 minutes. Taste, then adjust the seasoning if necessary.

Spoon as much of the fried rice as will fit into the pineapple shells and sprinkle with the cashew nuts and omelette strips. Garnish with the chillies and coriander leaves.

SERVES 4

Kiaw Naam Kung

Won Ton Soup with Prawns

Won tons are a Chinese-style stuffed noodle. Usually served in soups, they are easy to prepare, and with this light, fresh prawn filling won tons make a good meal in a bowl at any time of day. Chicken or fish are also suitable fillings.

225 g (8 oz) finely chopped prawns (shrimp)
6 garlic cloves, finely chopped
2 coriander (cilantro) roots, finely chopped
a sprinkle of ground white pepper
20 won ton sheets, 7.5 cm (3 in) square
1–2 tablespoons vegetable oil
935 ml (33 fl oz/3¾ cups) chicken or vegetable stock

2 tablespoons light soy sauce
4 raw prawns (shrimp), peeled and deveined
100 g (4 oz) Chinese cabbage or spinach leaves,
 roughly chopped
100 g (4 oz/1 cup) bean sprouts, tails removed
3 spring onions (scallions), slivered
ground white pepper, for sprinkling

In a bowl, combine the chopped prawns with one-third of the garlic, the coriander roots, ground pepper and a pinch of salt. Spoon 1 teaspoon of the mixture into the middle of each won ton sheet. Gather up, squeezing the corners together to make a little purse.

Heat the oil in a small wok or frying pan and stir-fry the remaining garlic until light golden. Remove from the heat and discard the garlic.

Heat a saucepan of water to boiling point. Gently drop each won ton into the water and cook for 2–3 minutes. Lift each won ton out with a slotted spoon and drop it into a bowl of warm water.

Heat the stock in a saucepan to boiling point. Add the light soy sauce, whole prawns and Chinese cabbage and cook for a few minutes.

Drain the cooked won tons and transfer them to the saucepan containing the stock.

Divide the bean sprouts among individual bowls and divide the won tons and the soup mixture among the bowls. Garnish with spring onions, ground pepper and the garlic oil.

SERVES 4

Far left: Spoon a small amount of the prawn mixture onto each won ton sheet.

Left: Gather up the won ton sheet, squeezing the corners together to make a purse.

Phat Ba-Mii Phak
Stir-fried Egg Noodles with Vegetables

2 tablespoons oyster sauce
1 tablespoon light soy sauce
1 teaspoon sugar
2 tablespoons vegetable oil
4 garlic cloves, finely chopped
225 g (8 oz) mixed Chinese broccoli florets, baby sweet
   corn, snake (yard-long) beans cut into lengths and
   snow peas (mangetout) cut into bite-sized pieces

250 g (9 oz) fresh egg noodles
45 g (1½ oz/½ cup) bean sprouts
3 spring onions (scallions), finely chopped
½ long red or green chilli, seeded and thinly sliced
a few coriander (cilantro) leaves, for garnish

Combine the oyster sauce, light soy sauce and sugar in a small bowl.

Heat the oil in a wok or frying pan and stir-fry the garlic over medium heat until lightly brown. Add all the mixed vegetables and stir-fry over high heat for 1–2 minutes.

Add the egg noodles and oyster sauce mixture to the wok and stir-fry for 2–3 minutes. Add the bean sprouts and spring onions. Taste, then adjust the seasoning if necessary.

Spoon onto a serving plate and garnish with the chilli and coriander leaves.

SERVES 4

Kuaytiaw Phat Khii Mao
Stir-fried Noodles with Holy Basil

450 g (1 lb) wide fresh flat rice noodles (sen yai)
2 teaspoons soy sauce
4 garlic cloves
4 bird's eye chillies, stems removed
4 tablespoons vegetable oil

200 g (7 oz) boneless, skinless chicken breast, cut into
   thin strips
2 tablespoons fish sauce
2 teaspoons palm sugar (jaggery)
½ bunch holy basil leaves

Put the noodles in a bowl with the soy sauce and rub the sauce through the noodles, separating them as you do so.

Pound the garlic and chillies together with a pestle and mortar until you have a fine paste.

Heat the oil in a wok, add the garlic and chilli paste and fry until fragrant. Add the chicken and toss until cooked. Add the fish sauce and palm sugar and cook until the sugar dissolves. Add the noodles and basil leaves, toss together and serve.

SERVES 4

PHAT WUN SEN
Hot and Sour Noodles with Prawns

200 g (7 oz) mung bean vermicelli
100 g (3 oz) minced (ground) pork
2 tablespoons oil
8 cooked prawns (shrimp), peeled and deveined
4 pickled garlic cloves, chopped
2 Asian shallots, thinly sliced

4 bird's eye chillies, thinly sliced
2 tablespoons fish sauce
1 tablespoon lime juice
2 tomatoes, seeded and cut into thin wedges
1/2 bunch Thai sweet basil leaves
1/2 bunch coriander (cilantro) leaves

Soak the noodles in hot water for 10 minutes, or until soft. Drain the noodles and cut them into shorter lengths using a pair of scissors.

Cook the pork in boiling water for 2 minutes, breaking it up into small pieces, then drain.

Heat the oil in a wok and add all the ingredients except the basil and coriander. Toss together for 1–2 minutes. Add the herbs, toss briefly and serve.

PICTURE ON PAGE 186   SERVES 4

KHAO PHAT KUNG NAAM PHRIK PHAO
Fried Rice with Prawns and Chilli Jam

225 g (8 oz) raw prawns (shrimp)
3 tablespoons vegetable oil
4 garlic cloves, finely chopped
1 small onion, sliced
3 teaspoons chilli jam (page 240)
450 g (1 lb) cooked jasmine rice, refrigerated overnight

1 tablespoon light soy sauce
1/2 teaspoon sugar
1 long red chilli, seeded and thinly sliced
2 spring onions (scallions), thinly sliced
ground white pepper, for sprinkling
a few coriander (cilantro) leaves, for garnish

Peel and devein the prawns and cut each prawn along the back so it opens like a butterfly (leave each prawn joined along the base and at the tail, leaving the tail attached).

Heat the oil in a wok or frying pan and stir-fry the garlic and onion over medium heat until light brown. Add the chilli jam and stir-fry for a few seconds until fragrant.

Add the prawns and stir-fry over high heat for 2 minutes, or until the prawns open and turn pink. Add the rice, light soy sauce and sugar and stir-fry for 3–4 minutes. Add the chilli and spring onions and mix well. Taste, then adjust the seasoning if necessary.

Spoon onto a serving place and sprinkle with the white pepper and coriander leaves.

SERVES 4

Hot and Sour Noodles with Prawns
(recipe on page 185)

Kung Lai Sai Krawk Nai Maw Din
Prawns and Sausage in a Clay Pot

Clay pot cooking is Chinese in style. If you have four smaller clay pots you can make individual dishes to serve instead of one large one. A heavy casserole will work just as well. The ingredients in the dish will flavour the rice as it cooks.

12 raw small prawns (shrimp), peeled, deveined and roughly chopped
1 lemon grass stalk, white part only, finely chopped
2 large green chillies, chopped
1 teaspoon Thai whisky or rice wine
1 teaspoon fish sauce
1 teaspoon tapioca flour
2 garlic cloves, chopped

2 coriander (cilantro) roots, chopped
2 cm (3/4 in) piece of ginger, chopped
2 Asian shallots, chopped
200 g (7 oz/1 cup) jasmine rice
2 tablespoons oil
2 Thai or Chinese sour sausages, thinly sliced
2 tablespoons chopped coriander (cilantro), for garnish

Put the prawns in a bowl with 1 tablespoon of lemon grass, the chillies, whisky, fish sauce and tapioca flour. Stir to combine.

Pound the remaining lemon grass with the garlic, coriander roots, ginger and shallots in a pestle and mortar or blend in a small food processor to form a rough paste.

Wash the rice in cold water until the water runs clear, then drain.

Heat the oil in a wok, add the garlic and lemon grass paste and cook for 3–4 minutes, stirring constantly. Add the drained rice and cook for 1 minute to coat the rice evenly in the mixture.

Transfer the rice to a large clay pot and add water so there is 2 cm (3/4 in) of water above the surface of the rice. Bring the water to a slow boil, then place the sausage slices on top of the rice and the prawn mixture on top of the sausages. Cover and cook over low heat for 15 minutes, or until the rice is cooked. Serve sprinkled with the coriander.

SERVES 4

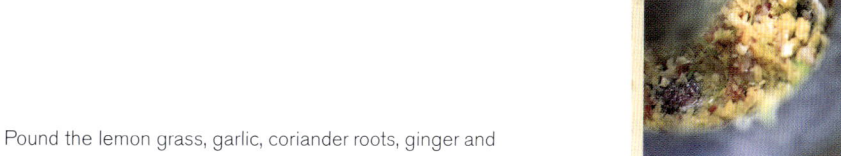

Pound the lemon grass, garlic, coriander roots, ginger and shallots into a paste.

PHAT KUAYTIAW RAAT NAA MUU
Stir-fried White Noodles with Pork

Noodles are enjoyed with fervour in Thailand. Large white noodles are used in this dish, which is one of the best-known noodle dishes, served at any time of the day or night. The light, bitter taste comes from the Chinese kale.

2 teaspoons oyster sauce

1½ tablespoons light soy sauce

1 teaspoon sugar

2 teaspoons yellow bean sauce

1 tablespoon tapioca flour

450 g (1 lb) wide fresh flat rice noodles (sen yai)

4 tablespoons vegetable oil

4–5 garlic cloves, finely chopped

225 g (8 oz) pork or boneless, skinless chicken breast, thinly sliced

175 g (6 oz) Chinese kale, cut into 2.5 cm (1 in) pieces, leaves separated

ground white pepper, for sprinkling

SEASONING

6 bird's eye chillies, sliced and mixed with 3 tablespoons white vinegar

3 tablespoons fish sauce

3 tablespoons roasted chilli powder

3 tablespoons sugar

Mix the oyster sauce, 1 tablespoon of the light soy sauce, sugar, yellow bean sauce and tapioca flour with 125 ml (4 fl oz/½ cup) water in a bowl.

Put the noodles in a bowl with the remaining soy sauce and rub the sauce through the noodles, separating them as you do so.

Heat 2 tablespoons oil in a wok or frying pan over medium heat and stir-fry the noodles for 4–5 minutes, or until they are browning at the edges and beginning to stick. Keep the noodles warm on a serving plate.

Heat the remaining oil in a wok or frying pan and stir-fry the garlic over medium heat until light brown. Add the pork and stir-fry for 2–3 minutes, or until the meat is cooked. Add the Chinese kale stalks and stir-fry for 1–2 minutes. Add the sauce and the Chinese kale leaves and stir for 1 minute. Taste and adjust the seasoning if necessary.

Spoon the pork and Chinese kale on top of the noodles and sprinkle with white pepper. Serve the seasoning ingredients in small bowls on the side, for adjusting the flavour.

SERVES 4

KHAO SAWY

Chiang Mai Noodles

One of Chiang Mai's well-known dishes, this is found on restaurant menus and at hawker stalls, particularly those near the mosque. Serve with the accompaniments suggested as they complement the noodles especially well.

PASTE
3 dried long red chillies
4 Asian shallots, chopped
4 garlic cloves, crushed
2 cm (3/4 in) piece of turmeric, grated
5 cm (2 in) piece of ginger, grated
4 tablespoons chopped coriander (cilantro) roots
1 teaspoon shrimp paste
1 teaspoon curry powder (page 243)

100 ml (4 fl oz) coconut cream (page 245)
2 tablespoons palm sugar (jaggery)
2 tablespoons soy sauce

4 chicken drumsticks and 4 chicken thighs, with skin and bone
500 ml (17 fl oz/2 cups) chicken stock or water
410 ml (14 fl oz/1 2/3 cups) coconut milk (page 245)
400 g (14 oz) fresh flat egg noodles
vegetable oil, for deep-frying
chopped or sliced spring onions (scallions), for garnish
a handful of coriander (cilantro) leaves, for garnish
lime wedges, to serve
pickled mustard greens or cucumber, to serve
roast chilli sauce (page 240), to serve
Asian shallots, quartered, to serve

To make the paste, soak the dried chillies in hot water for 10 minutes, then drain and chop the chillies into pieces, discarding the seeds. Put the chillies in a pestle and mortar with the shallots, garlic, turmeric, ginger, coriander roots and shrimp paste and pound to a fine paste. Add the curry powder and a pinch of salt and mix well.

Put the coconut cream in a wok or saucepan and simmer over medium heat for about 5 minutes, or until the cream separates and a layer of oil forms on the surface. Stir the cream if it starts to brown around the edges.

Add the paste and stir until fragrant. Add the sugar, soy sauce and chicken and stir well, then add the stock and coconut milk and bring to the boil. Reduce the heat and simmer for 30 minutes, or until the chicken is cooked and tender.

Meanwhile, cook 100 g (4 oz) of the egg noodles by deep-frying them in very hot oil in a saucepan until they puff up. Drain on paper towels. Cook the remaining noodles in boiling water according to the packet instructions.

Put the boiled noodles in a large bowl and spoon the chicken mixture over the top. Garnish with the crispy noodles, spring onions and coriander leaves. Serve the accompaniments alongside the chicken and noodles.

SERVES 4

Food Journey

RICE

Rice (khao) is not only the staple food of Thailand, it is a fundamental part of Thai life, integral to its culture and traditions. The greeting 'kin khao laew reu' means 'how are you?' but is translated as 'have you eaten rice yet?'. Rice is not just part of a meal, it is the meal. Other dishes are accompaniments.

The cultivation of rice may have started in Thailand. Wild rice originated somewhere in an area that now runs through Upper Assam, Burma, northern Thailand, South-West China and northern Vietnam, a fertile belt that is given over to rice cultivation today. The indigenous inhabitants of the area were cultivating rice in what would eventually become part of the kingdom of Thailand when most of China was still eating millet.

Rice became important to the Thai economy as it became a staple elsewhere. Arab and Indian traders took rice to India and the Middle East and the Chinese absorbed rice into the cuisine until it became their staple as well. Rice also travelled throughout Southeast Asia. Thailand is one of the world's major rice exporters and is self-sufficient in this staple food.

Most of the rice eaten in Thailand comes from local paddy. Originally, sticky rice was predominant but gradually long-grain rice became popular. Long-grain rice is served with every meal except snacks. A spoonful is usually eaten by itself before any other dish is added to it and it is never swamped with other food. Sticky rice is eaten by rolling some rice into a ball with one hand. It is then used to pick up food or to dip into a sauce. It is always eaten using your hand. Sticky rice is also used for desserts in both its white and 'black' forms.

The quality of rice is of paramount importance to the Thais. Jasmine rice, which has a flowery fragrance, is considered to be the best variety of long-grain. Rice is generally eaten within 12 and 18 months of harvesting. It is at its best after three months because when it is very new and still high in moisture, it is stickier. The drier rice becomes, the more water it needs to be cooked in.

Rice is cultivated in several different ways. An average crop takes between 100 and 200 days to mature depending on variety and growing climate. Rice can be grown in paddy fields – that is, in water – or in fields that are dry except for rainfall. Rice that relies on rainfall is mainly grown by hill tribes in northern Thailand. These farmers rotate their fields as the land becomes exhausted, cutting down new areas of jungle as they need them. Technology is relatively primitive in these areas and there are few labour-saving devices.

Paddy rice is grown either by sowing seed where the rice is to grow, or by initially growing the rice in small fields, where it can be nurtured, and then later transplanting it to larger fields. Paddy fields, which are sunken, with raised dams around them, are irrigated with water channels. The channels are filled by rainfall that is supplied by Thailand's monsoonal climate.

Ba-Mii Thaleh

Egg Noodles with Seafood

Ba-mii are wheat flour noodles, usually made with egg. Stalls specializing in ba-mii can be found all over Thailand – noodle dishes like this are usually eaten as a snack. Serve with sliced chillies in fish sauce, dried chilli and white sugar for seasoning.

8 raw prawns (shrimp)

2 squid tubes

4 scallops, cut in half horizontally

250 g (9 oz) egg noodles

1 tablespoon vegetable oil

4 Asian shallots, smashed with the side of a cleaver

4 spring onions (scallions), cut into lengths and smashed with the side of a cleaver

2 cm (^{3}/$_4$ in) piece of ginger, finely shredded

2 garlic cloves, thinly sliced

1 tablespoon preserved cabbage, rinsed and chopped (optional)

1 tablespoon oyster sauce

2 teaspoons soy sauce

2 teaspoons fish sauce

^{1}/$_2$ bunch holy basil leaves

Peel and devein the prawns and cut each prawn along the back so it opens like a butterfly (leave each prawn joined along the base and at the tail, leaving the tail attached).

Open out the squid tubes and score the insides in a crisscross pattern. Cut the squid into squares. Remove any dark veins from the scallops.

Cook the egg noodles in boiling water, then drain and rinse.

Heat the oil in a wok and add the shallots, spring onions, ginger, garlic and cabbage and stir-fry for 2 minutes. Add the prawns, squid and scallops one after the other, tossing after each addition, and cook for 3 minutes.

Add the oyster sauce, soy sauce and noodles and toss together. Add the fish sauce and holy basil, then serve.

SERVES 4

Score the insides of the squid tubes in a crisscross pattern.

MII KROB

Crispy Rice Noodles

This is made by deep-frying the thinnest rice noodles into light and crisp tangles. These are then tossed with sweet and sour sauce. This dish should be served as soon as it is cooked or the noodles will lose their crispiness.

75 g (3 oz) rice vermicelli noodles (sen mii)

vegetable oil, for deep-frying

200 g (7 oz) firm tofu (bean curd), cut into matchsticks

75 g (3 oz) small Asian shallots or small red onions, thinly sliced

150 g (6 oz) raw prawns (shrimp), peeled and deveined, tails intact

2 tablespoons fish sauce

2 tablespoons water or pickled garlic juice

1 tablespoon lime juice

2 tablespoons plum sauce (page 242) or tomato ketchup

1 tablespoon sweet chilli sauce (page 241)

4 tablespoons sugar

3 tablespoons palm sugar (jaggery)

3 small whole pickled garlic, thinly sliced

110 g (4 oz/1¼ cups) bean sprouts, tails removed, for garnish

3–4 spring onions (scallions), slivered, for garnish

1 long red chilli, seeded and cut into slivers, for garnish

Soak the noodles in cold water for 20 minutes, then drain and dry very thoroughly on paper towels. Cut them into short lengths with a pair of scissors.

Put the oil in the wok to a depth of about 10 cm (3 in) and heat over medium heat. Drop a piece of noodle into the wok. If the noodle sinks and then immediately floats and puffs, the oil is ready. Drop a small handful of the noodles into the oil. Turn them once (it only takes seconds) and remove them as soon as they have swelled and turned a dark ivory colour. Remove the noodles with a slotted spoon, hold over the wok briefly to drain, then drain on paper towels. Fry the remaining noodles in the same way. Break into smaller bits.

In the same oil, deep-fry the tofu for 7–10 minutes, or until golden and crisp. Remove and drain with a slotted spoon.

Deep-fry the shallots until crisp and golden brown. Remove with a slotted spoon and drain on paper towels.

Deep-fry the prawns for 1–2 minutes, or until they turn pink. Remove with a slotted spoon and drain on paper towels.

Carefully pour off all the oil from the wok. Add the fish sauce, water, lime juice, plum sauce, sweet chilli sauce, sugar and palm sugar to the wok and stir over low heat for 4–5 minutes, or until the sauce is slightly thick.

Add half of the rice noodles and toss gently, mixing them into the sauce. Add the remaining noodles and the tofu, prawns, pickled garlic and shallots, tossing for 1–2 minutes until coated. Spoon onto a platter and garnish with the bean sprouts, spring onions and chilli slivers.

SERVES 4

Chapter 9

VEGETABLES

Whether it's slivers of crisp, raw cucumber dipped in a spicy dressing or a speedily executed stir-fry, vegetable dishes rely on the freshest and best ingredients for texture and taste.

Naam Phrik Awng

Spicy Tomato Dipping Sauce

This famous dipping sauce from Chiang Mai should be served as a main course with blanched vegetables such as wedges of eggplant or cabbage, pieces of snake bean or pumpkin, and asparagus spears. Pieces of deep-fried pork skin are also suitable.

1 dried long red chilli

1 lemon grass stalk, white part only, thinly sliced

4 Asian shallots, finely chopped

2–3 garlic cloves, roughly chopped

½ teaspoon shrimp paste

1½ tablespoons vegetable oil

175 g (6 oz) minced (ground) fatty pork

450 g (1 lb) tomatoes, finely chopped

2 tablespoons fish sauce

1 tablespoon sugar

3 tablespoons tamarind purée

mixed vegetables, such as wedges of eggplant (aubergine), pieces of snake (yard-long) bean, wedges of cabbage, asparagus spears, baby corn, pieces of pumpkin (winter squash), to serve

a few coriander (cilantro) leaves, for garnish

pieces of pork skin, deep-fried, to serve

Slit the chilli lengthways with a sharp knife and discard all the seeds. Soak the chilli in hot water for 1–2 minutes, or until soft, then drain and chop roughly. Using a pestle and mortar, pound the chilli, lemon grass, shallots and garlic into a paste. Add the shrimp paste and mix well. Alternatively, use a small processor or blender to grind or blend the chilli, lemon grass, shallots, garlic and shrimp paste into a smooth paste.

Heat the oil in a saucepan or wok and stir-fry the paste over medium heat for 2 minutes, or until fragrant. Add the pork and stir for 2–3 minutes.

Add the tomatoes, fish sauce, sugar and tamarind purée. Reduce the heat and gently simmer for 25–30 minutes, or until the mixture is thick.

Blanch briefly any tough vegetables such as eggplant, snake beans, asparagus and pumpkin. Drain well.

Taste the sauce, then adjust with more tamarind, sugar or chilli if necessary. This dish should have three flavours: sweet, sour and lightly salted. Spoon into a bowl and garnish with the coriander. Serve with the vegetables and deep-fried pork skin.

SERVES 4

Phat Pak Ruam

Stir-fried Mixed Vegetables

Carrots, snow peas and asparagus are not typically Thai but are now widely grown and eaten. The north-west of Thailand has the right climate for growing colder-weather vegetables, particularly places like the king's project north of Chiang Mai.

4 thin asparagus spears
4 baby sweet corn
50 g (2 oz) snake (yard-long) beans
110 g (4 oz) mixed red and yellow capsicums (peppers)
1/2 small carrot
50 g (2 oz) Chinese broccoli or broccoli florets
25 g (1 oz) snow peas (mangetout), topped and tailed
2 cm (3/4 in) piece of ginger, thinly sliced

1 tablespoon fish sauce
1 1/2 tablespoons oyster sauce
2 tablespoons vegetable stock or water
1/2 teaspoon sugar
1 1/2 tablespoons vegetable oil
3–4 garlic cloves, finely chopped
2 spring onions (scallions), sliced

Cut off the tips of the asparagus and slice the stalks into 5 cm (2 in) lengths. Cut the baby sweet corn in halves lengthways and the beans into 2.5 cm (1 in) lengths. Cut both on an angle. Halve the capsicums and remove the seeds, then cut the flesh into bite-sized pieces. Peel the carrot and cut into batons.

Blanch the asparagus stalks, sweet corn, beans and broccoli in boiling salted water for 30 seconds. Transfer to a bowl of iced water to ensure a crisp texture, then drain and place in a bowl with the capsicum, carrot, snow peas, asparagus tips and sliced ginger.

Mix the fish sauce, oyster sauce, stock and sugar in a small bowl.

Heat the oil in a wok or frying pan and stir-fry the garlic over medium heat until light brown. Add all of the vegetables and the sauce mixture, then stir-fry over high heat for 2–3 minutes. Taste, then adjust the seasoning if necessary. Add the spring onions and toss.

SERVES 4

Vegetables for stir-fries should be cut into a uniform size.

NAAM PHRIK KA-PI

Shrimp Paste Dipping Sauce

Thai hot dipping sauce is used to accompany grilled or deep-fried fish, pieces of omelette, and fresh vegetables and fruit such as eggplant, cucumber, wing beans and snake beans. You can vary the number of chillies, depending on how hot you like it.

3–4 garlic cloves
2 teaspoons shrimp paste
2–3 small red and green chillies
3–4 Thai eggplants (aubergines) (optional)
1 teaspoon sugar
1 tablespoon fish sauce

2 tablespoons lime juice
mixed raw vegetables and fruit such as pieces of Thai
   eggplant (aubergine), cucumber batons, wing beans,
   pieces of snake (yard-long) bean, spring onions
   (scallions), pomelo segments, pieces of rose apple,
   to serve

Using a pestle and mortar, pound the garlic into a rough paste. Add the shrimp paste and grind together. Add the chillies and lightly bruise to release the hot taste. (Do this gently so the liquid won't splash.) Add the Thai eggplants and lightly pound. Add the sugar, fish sauce and lime juice and lightly mix in. Taste the sauce, then adjust the seasoning if necessary.

To make without a pestle and mortar, put the finely chopped garlic in a bowl and, using the back of a spoon, scrape the garlic into a paste. Add the

shrimp paste and mix well. Add the chillies and break them up with a fork. Add the Thai eggplants and squash them gently against the side of the bowl. Add the sugar, fish sauce and lime juice and lightly mix.

Spoon into a small serving bowl and serve with the mixed vegetables.

SERVES 4

Far left: Lightly pound the eggplants into the garlic, shrimp paste and chilli mixture.

Left: Squeeze in the lime juice and mix gently to combine.

Phat Phak Bung

Stir-fried Water Spinach

The vegetable that the Chinese call 'ong choy' is popular in Thailand where it's called 'phak bung'. It has long thin stalks and leafy tops, all of which are good to eat. Buy it from Asian supermarkets where it is sometimes called morning glory.

1½ tablespoons oyster sauce
1 teaspoon fish sauce
1 tablespoon yellow bean sauce
¼ teaspoon sugar

1½ tablespoons vegetable oil
2–3 garlic cloves, finely chopped
350 g (12 oz) water spinach, cut into 5 cm (2 in) lengths
1 red bird's eye chilli, slightly crushed (optional)

Mix the oyster sauce, fish sauce, yellow bean sauce and sugar in a small bowl.

Heat the oil in a wok or a frying pan and stir-fry the garlic over medium heat until light brown.

Increase the heat to very high, add the stalks of the water spinach and stir-fry for 1–2 minutes. Add the leaves of the water spinach, the sauce mixture and the chilli and stir-fry for another minute.

SERVES 4

Phat Chai Sim Naam-Man Hawy

Stir-fried Broccoli with Oyster Sauce

350 g (12 oz) Chinese broccoli, cut into pieces
1 tablespoon vegetable oil
2 garlic cloves, finely chopped

1 tablespoon oyster sauce
1 tablespoon light soy sauce

Blanch the Chinese broccoli in boiling salted water for 2–3 minutes, then drain thoroughly.

Heat the oil in a wok or frying pan and stir-fry the garlic over medium heat until light brown.

Add the Chinese broccoli and half of the oyster sauce and the light soy sauce. Stir-fry over high heat for 1–2 minutes, or until the stems are just tender. Drizzle with the remaining oyster sauce.

SERVES 4

Yam Tua Phuu

Wing Bean Salad

This is a fresh, crunchy salad that looks good on the table. Wing beans have four frilly edges and an interesting cross section when cut.

vegetable oil, for deep-frying
75 g (3 oz) Asian shallots, thinly sliced
175 g (6 oz) wing beans
55 g (2 oz) cooked chicken, shredded
1 lemon grass stalk, white part only, thinly sliced
2 tablespoons dried shrimp, ground

1½ tablespoons fish sauce
3–4 tablespoons lime juice
½ long red chilli or 1 small red chilli, finely chopped
55 g (2 oz) whole salted roasted peanuts
125 ml (4 fl oz/½ cup) coconut milk (page 245), to serve

Heat 2.5 cm (1 in) oil in a wok or deep frying pan over medium heat. Deep-fry the shallots for 3–4 minutes, or until they are light brown (without burning them). Lift out with a slotted spoon and drain on paper towels.

Slice the wing beans diagonally into thin pieces. Blanch in boiling water for 30 seconds, then drain and plunge into a bowl of cold water for

1–2 minutes. Drain and transfer to a bowl. Add the cooked chicken, lemon grass, dried shrimp, fish sauce, lime juice, chilli and half the peanuts. Mix with a spoon. Taste, then adjust the seasoning if necessary.

Put the wing bean salad in a serving bowl, drizzle with coconut milk and sprinkle with the shallots and the rest of the peanuts.

SERVES 4

PHAT FAK THAWNG KUB PHRIK
Pumpkin with Chilli and Basil

3 tablespoons dried shrimp
1/2 teaspoon shrimp paste
2 coriander (cilantro) roots
10–12 white peppercorns
2 garlic cloves, chopped
2 Asian shallots, chopped
125 ml (4 fl oz/1/2 cup) coconut cream (page 245)
300 g (11 oz) butternut pumpkin (squash), cut into
  4 cm (1 1/2 in) cubes

2 large red chillies, cut lengthways
125 ml (4 fl oz/1/2 cup) coconut milk (page 245)
1 tablespoon fish sauce
1 tablespoon palm sugar (jaggery)
2 teaspoons lime juice
12 Thai sweet basil leaves

Soak 2 tablespoons of the dried shrimp in a small bowl of water for 20 minutes, then drain.

Put the remaining dried shrimp, shrimp paste, coriander roots, white peppercorns, garlic and shallots in a pestle and mortar or food processor and pound or blend to a paste.

Bring the coconut cream to the boil in a saucepan and simmer for 5 minutes. Add the paste and stir to combine. Cook for another 2–3 minutes, then add the pumpkin, chillies, rehydrated shrimp and coconut milk. Stir to combine all the ingredients and simmer for 10–15 minutes, until the pumpkin is just tender. Don't let the pumpkin turn to mush.

Add the fish sauce, palm sugar and lime juice to the pan and cook for another 2–3 minutes. Stir in the basil leaves before serving.

SERVES 4

PHAT MA-KHEUA

Baby Eggplant and Cherry Tomato Stir-fry

Although a mixture of Thai eggplants of different colours will make this dish more visually appealing, just one type will do fine. The eggplants may discolour when you cook them but don't worry as the flavour won't be affected.

12 small round Thai eggplants (aubergines), green, yellow or purple
1 teaspoon fish sauce, plus 1 tablespoon
1 tablespoon vegetable oil
1 small red chilli, chopped
1 tablespoon thinly sliced ginger

2 Asian shallots, finely chopped
1 garlic clove, chopped
150 g (6 oz) cherry tomatoes
2 tablespoons black vinegar
2 tablespoons palm sugar (jaggery)
12–18 Thai sweet basil leaves

Cut each eggplant in half and toss them in a bowl with 1 teaspoon fish sauce. Put about 8 cm (3 in) of water in a wok and bring to the boil. Place the eggplants in a bamboo steamer, place the steamer over the boiling water and steam the eggplants for 15 minutes.

Heat the oil in a wok, add the red chilli, ginger, shallots and garlic and cook for 15 seconds. Add the eggplants and tomatoes and toss well. Add the black vinegar, sugar and remaining fish sauce and cook for 2–3 minutes, until the sauce thickens. Stir in the basil leaves and serve.

SERVES 4

PHAT THUA FAK YAO

Stir-fried Snake Beans

2 tablespoons vegetable oil
2 teaspoons red curry paste (page 236) or bought paste
350 g (12 oz) boneless, skinless chicken breast, thinly sliced

350 g (12 oz) snake (yard-long) beans, cut diagonally into 2.5 cm (1 in) pieces
1 tablespoon fish sauce
25 g (1 oz) sugar
4 makrut (kaffir) lime leaves, very finely shredded

Heat the oil in a wok or frying pan and stir-fry the curry paste over medium heat for 2 minutes, or until fragrant. Add the chicken and stir-fry for 4–5 minutes, or until the chicken is cooked.

Add the beans, fish sauce and sugar. Stir-fry for another 4–5 minutes. Transfer to a serving plate and sprinkle with the makrut lime leaves.

SERVES 4

Chapter 10

DESSERTS

The balance of sweet, salty and sour flavours is as evident in desserts as it is in other parts of a meal. Rice and fresh fruit are often used. Desserts are served as snacks from roadside stalls.

THAPTHIM KRAWP

Crisp Rubies

Crisp rubies resemble jewel-like pieces of pomegranate. The combination of ingredients may sound somewhat odd, but crisp rubies are very popular and are actually quite delicious, especially when served with ice and coconut cream.

8–10 drops of pink or red food colouring
2 x 225 g (8 oz) tins water chestnuts, drained and each
    chestnut cut into 10–12 pieces
150 g (6 oz) tapioca flour

250 g (9 oz/1 cup) sugar
185 ml (6 fl oz/¾ cup) coconut milk (page 245)
¼ teaspoon salt
crushed ice, to serve

Add the food colouring to 60 ml (2 fl oz/¼ cup) water in a bowl. Add the water chestnuts and mix with a spoon. Leave for 10 minutes, or until the pieces turn pink, then drain and leave to dry.

Put the tapioca flour in a plastic bag. Add the pink water chestnuts and shake the bag to coat well. Dust off any excess flour. Heat a saucepan of water to boiling point. Add half of the water chestnuts and cook for 1–2 minutes, or until they float to the surface. Lift out with a slotted spoon and put them in a bowl of cold water. Repeat with the remaining water chestnuts. Drain all the pieces.

In a small saucepan, heat 250 ml (9 fl oz/1 cup) water and the sugar until the mixture boils, stirring constantly. Lower the heat to medium and simmer for 5–10 minutes, or until reduced to a thick syrup.

Mix the coconut milk and salt in a small saucepan and cook over medium heat for 1–2 minutes, or until slightly creamy.

Divide the water chestnuts among individual bowls and top with a few spoonfuls each of sugar syrup and creamy coconut milk. Sprinkle with ice and serve cold.

SERVES 6

When you have coloured and floured the water chestnuts, cook them in two batches. When they float, lift them out.

Khao Niaw Dam

Black Sticky Rice with Taro

Vegetables like taro are often used in Thai desserts. Black sticky rice is simply white rice with the bran left on and it is actually more purple than black. You must cook the rice before adding any sugar or it will toughen and never become tender.

175 g (6 oz) black sticky rice (black glutinous rice)
280 g (10 oz) taro, cut into 1 cm (½ in) squares and
   soaked in cold water

150 g (6 oz) palm sugar (jaggery)
1 teaspoon salt
185 ml (6 fl oz/¾ cup) coconut milk (page 245)

Put the rice in a bowl and pour in cold water to come 5 cm (2 in) above the rice. Soak for at least 3 hours, or overnight if possible.

Drain the rice and add clean water. Scoop the rice through your fingers four or five times to clean it, then drain. Repeat two or three times with clean water to remove the unwanted starch. (The water will never be completely clear when using black rice, even when all the unwanted starch has gone.)

Put the rice in a saucepan with 625 ml (22 fl oz/ 2½ cups) cold water. Bring to the boil, stirring the rice frequently as it reaches boiling point. Reduce the heat to medium. Stir, then simmer for 30–35 minutes, or until the rice is cooked and nearly all of the liquid has been absorbed. The rice should be very moist, but with hardly any water remaining in the bottom of the saucepan.

Meanwhile, drain the taro, spread it on a plate and transfer it to a bamboo steamer or other steamer. Taking care not to burn your hands, set the basket over a pan of boiling water over high heat. Cover and steam for 8–10 minutes, or until the taro is cooked and tender.

When the rice is cooked, add the sugar and gently stir until the sugar has dissolved. Add the taro and gently mix.

Mix the salt into the coconut milk. Divide the rice mixture among individual bowls and drizzle the coconut milk on top. Serve warm.

SERVES 6

Black sticky rice is commonly used for desserts and, when cooked, is actually a dark purplish-red.

SANGKAYA

Custards

The classic custard cooked in a pumpkin is one of many popular custards in Thailand. As here, coconut, sweet potato, jackfruit and taro are also used as flavourings. Serve in banana leaves, as shown, or pour the mixture into baby pumpkins.

banana leaves
80 ml (3 fl oz/⅓ cup) coconut milk (page 245)
7 eggs
275 g (10 oz) palm sugar (jaggery), cut into small pieces
¼ teaspoon salt

5–6 fresh pandanus leaves, dried and cut into small pieces, bruised, or 3 teaspoons natural vanilla extract
100 g (4 oz) young coconut meat, cut into small pieces, or orange sweet potato, jackfruit or taro, cut into matchsticks

To soften the banana leaves and prevent them from splitting, put them in a hot oven for about 10–20 seconds, or blanch them briefly. Cut the banana leaves into 12 circles about 13 cm (5 in) in diameter with the fibre running lengthways.

Place one circle with the fibre running lengthways and another on top with the fibre running across. Make a 1 cm (½ in) deep tuck 4 cm (1½ in) long (4 cm in from the edge and no further) and pin securely with a small sharp toothpick. Repeat this at the opposite point and at the two side points, making four tucks altogether. Flatten the base as best you can. Repeat to make six cups. Alternatively, use a small shallow rectangular cake tin.

Combine the coconut milk, eggs, palm sugar, salt and pandanus leaves in a bowl, using a spoon, for 10 minutes, or until the sugar has dissolved. Pour the custard through a sieve into a bowl and discard the pandanus leaves.

Add the coconut, orange sweet potato, jackfruit or taro to the custard and lightly mix. Spoon the mixture into each banana leaf cup, filling to 1 cm (½ in) from the top.

Half fill a wok or a steamer pan with water, cover and bring to a rolling boil over high heat. Place the custard cups on a plate. Use a plate that will fit on the rack of a traditional bamboo steamer basket or on a steamer rack inside the wok or steamer pan. Taking care not to burn your hands, place the plate on the bamboo steamer or steamer rack inside the wok or pan. Cover, reduce the heat to low and cook for 10–15 minutes. Check and replenish the water after 10 minutes. Serve the custards at room temperature or chilled. They can be covered and refrigerated for up to three or four days before serving.

MAKES 6

Ice Cream Kra Ti
Coconut Ice Cream

400 ml (14 fl oz/1 2/3 cups) coconut milk (page 245)
250 ml (9 fl oz/1 cup) thick (double/heavy) cream
2 eggs

4 egg yolks
160 g (6 oz/2/3 cup) caster (superfine) sugar
1/4 teaspoon salt

Pour the coconut milk and cream into a medium saucepan. Stir over gentle heat without boiling for 2–3 minutes. Remove from the heat, cover and keep warm over a bowl of boiling water.

Put the eggs, egg yolks, sugar and salt in a large heatproof bowl. Beat with electric beaters for 3 minutes, or until frothy and thickened.

Place the bowl over a pan of simmering water. Continue to beat the egg mixture, slowly adding all the coconut mixture until the custard thickens slightly. This process will take 8–10 minutes. The mixture should be a thin cream and easily coat the back of a spoon. Do not boil it or it will curdle. Set aside until cool. Stir the mixture occasionally while it is cooling. Pour into a freezer box or churn in an ice cream machine. If you are using a freezer box, take the mixture out of the freezer and beat it with electric beaters at least twice during the freezing. You want it to get plenty of air whipped into it. Cover and freeze completely. To serve, remove from the freezer for 10–15 minutes, until slightly softened. Serve in scoops with slices of coconut.

SERVES 10

Khao Niaw Mamuang
Sticky Rice with Mango

In Thailand the mango season is in April. Some mangoes taste better when green, crisp and crunchy, others when they are ripe. Either way, there is a lot of variety and many different flavours. This sticky rice with mango is arguably the best Thai dessert.

4 large ripe mangoes
1 quantity of steamed sticky rice with coconut milk (page 247)

170 ml (6 fl oz/2/3 cup) coconut cream (page 245) mixed with 1/4 teaspoon salt, for garnish
2 tablespoons dry-fried mung beans (optional)

Peel the mangoes and slice off two outside cheeks of each, removing as much flesh as you can in large pieces. Avoid cutting very close to the stone where the flesh is fibrous. Discard the stone. Slice each cheek lengthways into four or five pieces.

Arrange the mango pieces on a serving plate. Spoon a portion of the sticky rice near the mango slices. Spoon the coconut cream garnish on top and sprinkle with the fried mung beans. Serve at room temperature.

SERVES 4

Saku Peak Kab Ma Prao On
Tapioca Pudding with Young Coconut

170 ml (6 fl oz/^{2}/$_3$ cup) coconut milk (page 245)
^{3}/$_4$ teaspoon salt
110 g (4 oz) tapioca or sago
6 pandanus leaves

60 g (2 oz/^{1}/$_4$ cup) caster (superfine) sugar
150 g (6 oz) young coconut meat in syrup (from a tin), drained

In a small bowl, stir the coconut milk with ^{1}/$_2$ teaspoon salt until combined.

Bring 1 litre (35 fl oz/4 cups) water to a rolling boil in a saucepan. Add the tapioca and pandanus leaves and stir occasionally with a wooden spoon for 15–20 minutes while simmering over medium heat. Stir until all the grains are swollen, clear and shiny. Reduce the heat if necessary. Add the sugar and ^{1}/$_4$ teaspoon salt to the saucepan and stir until the sugar has dissolved. The tapioca should now be almost cooked. Add the coconut meat and gently mix. Remove the pandanus leaves. Leave to thicken for 5 minutes before dividing among individual bowls. Drizzle coconut milk on top. Serve warm.

SERVES 4

Kluay Buat Chii
Banana in Coconut Cream

There are more than 20 varieties of banana in Thailand, all of which are used in cooking. Use nice sweet bananas for this recipe and avoid particularly large ones.

400 ml (14 fl oz/1^2/$_3$ cups) coconut milk (page 245)
4 tablespoons sugar

5 just-ripe bananas
^{1}/$_2$ teaspoon salt

Put the coconut milk and sugar in a saucepan. Add 125 ml (4 fl oz/^{1}/$_2$ cup) water and bring to the boil. Reduce the heat and simmer until the sugar dissolves.

Peel the bananas and cut them into 5 cm (2 in) lengths. If you are using very small bananas, leave them whole.

When the sugar in the coconut milk has dissolved, add the bananas and salt. Cook gently over low to medium heat for 5 minutes, or until the bananas are soft.

Divide the bananas and coconut cream among four bowls. Serve warm or at room temperature.

SERVES 4

SWEETS

ﾟｏﾟｏﾟｏﾟｏﾟｏﾟｏﾟｏﾟｏﾟｏﾟｏﾟｏﾟｏﾟｏﾟｏﾟｏﾟｏﾟｏﾟｏﾟｏﾟ

People in Thailand use the term khwang waan, literally meaning sweet stuff, to refer to anything that is sweet, including desserts, sweet snacks or sweets themselves. Most khwang waan are eaten as snacks rather than as desserts but nevertheless meals can be finished on a sweet note.

In Thailand sweet things have always been part of the cuisine, originally made with crushed beans, coconut, rice, sugar and fruit. These were supplemented with the use of eggs and pastry, ideas that arrived with the Portuguese. Even more recently, ice cream has become popular.

Thai sweets differ from European ones in both texture and flavour. Though egg custards and pastries may be reminiscent of European desserts, they are often much sweeter. Unlike in Europe, salt is used as a flavour in coconut desserts and sweets, to offset sweetness. Flower and leaf perfumes such as jasmine and pandanus are used in sugar syrups. Favourite textures include jellies, custards and sticky, chewy ingredients like rice.

Often combinations of textures are eaten together, particularly in desserts like 'green strings' where 'strings' made of green dough are served with crushed ice, sugar syrup and coconut juice. Colours come from pandanus (green), egg yolks (yellow), and coconut ash and sesame (black). Crunch is often added with the use of lotus seeds, beans, sweet corn kernels and water chestnuts. Fruit is eaten fresh and is also candied and preserved.

Some sweets are associated with ceremonies and in many cases are thought to sweeten the gods. Other sweets are eaten at particular times of the year, such as ash pudding at Thai New Year, and sticky rice with banana at the end of Thai Lent.

Phetchaburi province is famous for its sweets. It is also the land of the palm tree. Both coconut and sugar palms supply the sweet-makers with raw ingredients to ply their trade. Coconut is used both fresh and dried. When fresh, the flesh is soft and jelly-like with lots of liquid inside and these coconuts are sold for drinking. Older, drier coconut flesh, however, is shredded and used as a garnish. Coconut is used to flavour sticky rice, which is steamed in leaves. Palm sugar (jaggery) comes in different grades, the best being from Phetchaburi province. It is usually sold in discs or log shapes, although softer types can come in tubs. Palm sugar is used to sweeten Thai-style waffles and used in perfumed syrups for 'wet' and layered sweets.

Ice Cream Mamuang
Mango Sorbet

3 ripe mangoes
150 g (6 oz) palm sugar (jaggery)

zest and juice from 1 lime

Peel the mangoes and cut the flesh off the stones. Chop into small pieces. Put the sugar and 185 ml (6 fl oz/³⁄₄ cup) water in a saucepan and bring to the boil. Reduce the heat and simmer until the liquid reduces by half. Put the sugar syrup, mango and lime zest and juice in a food processor or blender and whiz until smooth.

Pour into a freezer box or churn in an ice cream machine. If you are using a freezer box, take the mixture out of the freezer and beat it with electric beaters at least twice during the freezing time. You want it to have plenty of air whipped into it or it will be too icy and hard. Cover and freeze the sorbet completely.

SERVES 4

Kluay Thawt
Deep-fried Bananas

BATTER
125 g (5 oz/1 cup) self-raising flour
¹⁄₂ teaspoon baking powder
2 teaspoons sugar
¹⁄₄ teaspoon salt
25 g (1 oz) grated coconut (page 245) or
   desiccated coconut

2 tablespoons sesame seeds
350 ml (12 fl oz/1¹⁄₃ cups) water, at room temperature

vegetable oil, for deep-frying
4 ripe bananas

Put the flour, baking powder, sugar, salt, coconut and sesame seeds in a bowl. Add the water and lightly mix with a spoon or fork until smooth.

Heat 7.5 cm (3 in) oil in a wok or deep-frying pan over medium heat. When the oil seems hot, drop a little batter into the oil. If it sizzles immediately, the oil is ready. It is important not to have the oil too hot or the batter will burn.

Halve the bananas lengthways, then cut them into 5 cm (2 in) chunks. Preheat the oven to 150°C (300°F/Gas 2). Dip the banana chunks one at a time into the batter, then lower into the hot oil. Deep-fry about 5 pieces at a time for 3–4 minutes, or until golden, then lift out with a slotted spoon or a pair of chopsticks. Drain on paper towels and keep warm in the oven. Transfer to a serving plate and serve warm.

SERVES 4

SANGKAYA FAK THAWNG

Pumpkin with Custard

This traditional Thai dessert, made with coconut milk and palm or coconut sugar, is sweet and rich in taste. Choose honey-coloured pumpkins, either one small to medium, or four very small ones. When cooked and cooled, cut them into wedges for serving.

1 small to medium or 4 small pumpkins (winter squash)
2 tablespoons coconut milk (page 245)
2 eggs

150 g (6 oz) palm sugar (jaggery), cut into small pieces
2–3 pandanus leaves, dried and cut into small pieces, and bruised, or 1 teaspoon natural vanilla extract

Carefully cut off the top of the pumpkin. Try not to pierce the pumpkin at any other point with the knife as it is more likely to crack or leak around such punctures. Using a spoon, scrape out and discard all the seeds and fibres.

To make a custard, stir the coconut milk, eggs, palm sugar, pandanus leaves and a pinch of salt in a bowl, using a spoon, for 10 minutes, or until the sugar has dissolved. Pour the custard through a sieve into a measuring cup. Discard the pandanus leaves. Pour the custard into the pumpkin shell, filling to within 2.5 cm (1 in) of the top.

Fill a wok or a steamer pan with water, cover and bring to a rolling boil over high heat. Place the pumpkin on a plate. Use a plate that will fit on the rack of a traditional bamboo steamer basket or on

a steamer rack inside the wok. Taking care not to burn your hands, place the plate on the rack or steamer inside the wok. Cover, reduce the heat to low and cook for 30–45 minutes, or until the pumpkin is cooked and the custard puffed up. Check and replenish the water every 10 minutes.

Turn off the heat and remove the cover. Carefully remove the pumpkin and set aside to cool. If you prefer, you can leave the pumpkin in the steamer to cool to room temperature.

Cut the pumpkin into thick wedges for serving. Serve at room temperature or chilled.

As an alternative, you can steam the mixture in a shallow cake tin, and serve it in spoonfuls on top of steamed sticky rice with coconut milk (page 247).

SERVES 4

Right: Strain the custard to remove the pandanus leaves.

Far right: Pour the custard into the pumpkin shells.

BASICS

Fragrant curry pastes and curry powder, spicy and sour dipping sauces, freshly squeezed coconut milk and cream, and perfect steamed or sticky rice – here are the essential recipes for authentic Thai cuisine.

Khreuang Kaeng Phet
Red Curry Paste

3–4 dried long red chillies, about 13 cm (5 in) long
10 dried or fresh small red chillies, about 5 cm (2 in) long
2 lemon grass stalks, white part only, thinly sliced
2.5 cm (1 in) piece of galangal, thinly sliced
1 teaspoon very finely chopped makrut (kaffir) lime skin
  or makrut lime leaves

4–5 garlic cloves, finely chopped
3–4 Asian shallots, finely chopped
5–6 coriander (cilantro) roots, finely chopped
2 teaspoons shrimp paste
1 teaspoon ground coriander, dry-roasted

Slit the chillies in half lengthways and discard the seeds. Soak the dried chillies in hot water for 1–2 minutes, or until soft. Drain and roughly chop.

Using a pestle and mortar, pound the chillies, lemon grass, galangal and makrut lime skin or leaves into a paste. Add the remaining ingredients and pound until the mixture forms a smooth paste. Alternatively, use a food processor or blender to grind or blend the ingredients into a paste. Add cooking oil, as needed, to assist the blending.

Store the paste in an airtight jar for two weeks in the refrigerator or two months in a freezer.

MAKES 125 G (5 OZ/½ CUP)

Khreuang Kaeng Matsaman
Massaman Curry Paste

2 dried long red chillies, about 13 cm (5 in) long
1 lemon grass stalk, white part only, thinly sliced
2.5 cm (1 in) piece of galangal, finely chopped
5 cloves
10 cm (4 in) piece of cinnamon stick, crushed
10 cardamom seeds

½ teaspoon freshly grated nutmeg
6 garlic cloves, finely chopped
4 Asian shallots, finely chopped
4–5 coriander (cilantro) roots, finely chopped
1 teaspoon shrimp paste

Slit the chillies in half lengthways and discard the seeds. Soak the dried chillies in hot water for 1–2 minutes, or until soft. Drain and roughly chop.

Using a pestle and mortar, pound the chillies, lemon grass, galangal and spices into a paste. Add the garlic, shallots and coriander roots. Pound and mix together. Add the shrimp paste and then pound until the mixture forms a smooth paste. Alternatively, use a food processor or blender to grind or blend the ingredients into a paste. Add cooking oil, as needed, to assist the blending.

Store the paste in an airtight jar for two weeks in the refrigerator or two months in a freezer.

MAKES 250 G (9 OZ/1 CUP)

Khreuang Kaeng Hangleh
Chiang Mai Curry Paste

1 tablespoon coriander seeds, dry-roasted
2 teaspoons cumin seeds, dry-roasted
2 dried long red chillies, about 13 cm (5 in) long
1/2 teaspoon salt
5 cm (2 in) piece of galangal, grated
1 lemon grass stalk, white part only, finely chopped

2 Asian shallots, chopped
2 garlic cloves, chopped
1 teaspoon grated turmeric or a pinch of ground turmeric
1 teaspoon shrimp paste
1/2 teaspoon ground cassia or cinnamon

Grind the coriander seeds to a powder with a pestle and mortar. Grind the cumin seeds.

Slit the chillies in half lengthways and discard the seeds. Soak the dried chillies in hot water for 1–2 minutes, or until soft. Drain and roughly chop.

Using a pestle and mortar, pound the chillies, salt, galangal, lemon grass, shallots, garlic and turmeric to as smooth a paste as possible. Add the shrimp paste, ground coriander, cumin and cassia and pound until the mixture forms a smooth paste. Alternatively, use a food processor or blender to grind or blend the ingredients into a paste. Add cooking oil, as needed, to assist the blending.

MAKES 185 G (7 OZ/3/4 CUP)

Khreuang Kaeng Phanaeng
Dry Curry Paste

2 dried long red chillies, about 13 cm (5 in) long
2 lemon grass stalks, white part only, thinly sliced
2.5 cm (1 in) piece of galangal, finely chopped
4–5 garlic cloves, finely chopped
3–4 Asian shallots, finely chopped

5–6 coriander (cilantro) roots, finely chopped
1 teaspoon shrimp paste
1 teaspoon ground cumin, dry-roasted
3 tablespoons unsalted peanuts, chopped

Slit the chillies in half lengthways and discard the seeds. Soak the dried chillies in hot water for 1–2 minutes, or until soft. Drain and roughly chop.

Using a pestle and mortar, pound the chillies, lemon grass and galangal into a paste. Add the remaining ingredients one at a time and pound until the mixture forms a very smooth paste. Alternatively, use a food processor or blender to grind or blend the ingredients into a paste. Add cooking oil, as needed, to assist the blending.

Store the paste in an airtight jar for two weeks in the refrigerator or two months in a freezer.

MAKES 80 G (3 OZ/1/3 CUP)

Khreuang Kaeng Khiaw-Waan
Green Curry Paste

8–10 small green chillies, seeded
2 lemon grass stalks, white part only, thinly sliced
2.5 cm (1 in) piece of galangal, finely chopped
1 teaspoon very finely chopped makrut (kaffir) lime skin
   or makrut lime leaves
4–5 garlic cloves, finely chopped

3–4 Asian shallots, chopped
5–6 coriander (cilantro) roots, finely chopped
a handful of holy basil leaves, finely chopped
2 teaspoons shrimp paste
1 teaspoon ground coriander, dry-roasted
1 teaspoon ground cumin, dry-roasted

Using a pestle and mortar, pound the chillies, lemon grass, galangal and makrut lime skin or leaves into a paste. Add the garlic, shallots and coriander roots and pound together. Add the remaining ingredients one at a time and pound until the mixture forms a smooth paste.

Alternatively, use a food processor or blender to grind or blend the ingredients into a paste. Add cooking oil, as needed, to assist the blending.

Store the paste in an airtight jar for two weeks in the refrigerator or two months in a freezer.

PICTURE ON OPPOSITE PAGE

MAKES 125 G (5 OZ/½ CUP)

Khreuang Kaeng Leuang
Yellow Curry Paste

3 teaspoons coriander seeds, dry-roasted
1 teaspoon cumin seeds, dry-roasted
2–3 dried long red chillies
2 lemon grass stalks, white part only, thinly sliced
3 Asian shallots, finely chopped

2 garlic cloves, finely chopped
2 tablespoons grated turmeric or 1 teaspoon
   ground turmeric
1 teaspoon shrimp paste

Grind the coriander seeds to a powder with a pestle and mortar. Grind the cumin seeds.

Slit the chillies in half lengthways and discard the seeds. Soak the dried chillies in hot water for 1–2 minutes, or until soft. Drain and roughly chop.

Using a pestle and mortar, pound the chillies, lemon grass, shallots, garlic and turmeric to as

smooth a paste as possible. Add the shrimp paste, ground coriander and cumin and pound until the mixture forms a smooth paste. Alternatively, use a food processor or blender to grind or blend the ingredients into a paste. Add cooking oil, as needed, to assist the blending.

Store the paste in an airtight jar for two weeks in the refrigerator or two months in a freezer.

MAKES 250 G (9 OZ/1 CUP)

Naam Jaew
Chilli Jam

oil, for frying
20 Asian shallots, sliced
10 garlic cloves, sliced
3 tablespoons dried shrimp
7 dried long red chillies, chopped

3 tablespoons tamarind purée or 3 tablespoons
   lime juice
6 tablespoons palm sugar (jaggery)

1 teaspoon shrimp paste

Heat the oil in a wok or saucepan. Fry the shallots and garlic together until golden, then transfer from the wok to a blender or food processor.

Fry the dried shrimp and chillies for 1–2 minutes, then add these to the blender along with the remaining ingredients. Blend with as much of the frying oil as necessary to make a paste that you can pour. Put the paste back in the clean saucepan and bring to the boil. Reduce the heat and simmer until thick. Be careful because if you overcook this you will end up with a caramelized lump. Season the sauce with salt or fish sauce.

Chilli jam is used as a base for recipes, especially stir-fries, as well as a seasoning or accompaniment. It will keep for several months in an airtight jar in the refrigerator.

MAKES 250 G (9 OZ/1 CUP)

Naam Phrik Phao
Roast Chilli Sauce

80 ml (3 fl oz/⅓ cup) oil
2 Asian shallots, finely chopped
2 garlic cloves, finely chopped

40 g (1½ oz) dried chilli flakes
¼ teaspoon palm sugar (jaggery)

Heat the oil in a small saucepan and fry the shallots and garlic until brown. Add the chilli flakes and palm sugar and stir well. Season with a pinch of salt.

Use as a dipping sauce or accompaniment. The sauce can be stored in a jar in the refrigerator for several weeks.

MAKES 185 G (7 OZ/¾ CUP)

NAAM JIM KAI
Sweet Chilli Sauce

7 long red chillies, seeded and roughly chopped
185 ml (6 fl oz/³⁄₄ cup) white vinegar

8 tablespoons sugar
¹⁄₂ teaspoon salt

Using a pestle and mortar or a small blender, pound or blend the chillies into a rough paste.

Put the white vinegar, sugar and salt in a small saucepan and bring to the boil over high heat, stirring constantly. Reduce the heat to medium and simmer for 15–20 minutes, until the mixture forms a thick syrup. Spoon the chilli paste into the syrup and cook for 1–2 minutes, then pour into a bowl ready to serve.

MAKES 60 ML (2 FL OZ/¼ CUP)

NAAM JIM AAHAAN THALEH
Garlic and Chilli Sauce

4 garlic cloves, finely chopped
3 bird's eye chillies, mixed red and green, stems removed, lightly crushed

2 tablespoons lime juice
1 tablespoon fish sauce
1 teaspoon sugar

Put the garlic, chillies, lime juice, fish sauce and sugar in a small bowl. Mix together.

The sauce can be stored in a jar in the refrigerator for several weeks.

MAKES 125 ML (4 FL OZ/½ CUP)

Naam Jim Plum
Plum Sauce

185 ml (6 fl oz/³/4 cup) white vinegar
8 tablespoons sugar

1 preserved plum (available in jars) without liquid

Put the white vinegar and sugar in a small saucepan and bring to the boil over high heat, stirring constantly. Reduce the heat to medium and simmer for 15–20 minutes, until the mixture forms a thick syrup.

Add the preserved plum to the syrup and mash it with a spoon or fork. Cook for 1–2 minutes to form a smooth paste, then pour into a bowl ready to serve.

MAKES 60 ML (2 FL OZ/¼ CUP)

Naam Sa-Te
Peanut Sauce

1 tablespoon oil
2 garlic cloves, crushed
4 Asian shallots, finely chopped
1 lemon grass stalk, white part only, finely chopped
2 teaspoons Thai curry powder (page 243) or
   bought powder

1 tablespoon tamarind purée
1 tablespoon chilli paste
160 g (6 oz/1 cup) unsalted roasted peanuts,
   roughly chopped
375 ml (13 fl oz/1½ cups) coconut milk (page 245)
2 teaspoons palm sugar (jaggery)

Heat the oil in a saucepan and fry the garlic, shallots and lemon grass for 1 minute. Add the Thai curry powder and stir until fragrant. Add the remaining ingredients and bring slowly to

the boil. Add enough boiling water to make a spoonable sauce and simmer for 2 minutes. Season with salt to taste.

MAKES 375 G (13 OZ/1½ CUPS)

Ajat
Cucumber Relish

80 ml (3 fl oz/$\frac{1}{3}$ cup) rice vinegar
125 g (5 oz/$\frac{1}{2}$ cup) sugar
1 small red chilli, seeded and chopped
1 teaspoon fish sauce

80 g (3 oz/$\frac{1}{2}$ cup) peanuts, lightly roasted and
  roughly chopped
1 Lebanese cucumber, unpeeled, seeded, finely diced

Put the vinegar and sugar in a small saucepan with 125 ml (4 fl oz/$\frac{1}{2}$ cup) of water. Bring to the boil, then reduce the heat and simmer for 5 minutes.

Allow to cool before stirring in the chopped chilli, fish sauce, peanuts and cucumber.

MAKES 185 G (7 OZ/$\frac{3}{4}$ CUP)

Phong Karii
Curry Powder

1 tablespoon black peppercorns
2 teaspoons white peppercorns
1 tablespoon cloves
3 tablespoons coriander seeds
3 tablespoons cumin seeds

1 tablespoon fennel seeds
seeds from 8 cardamom pods
3 tablespoons dried chilli flakes
2 tablespoons ground ginger
3 tablespoons ground turmeric

Dry-roast the black and white peppercorns, cloves, coriander seeds, cumin seeds and fennel seeds, one ingredient at a time, in a frying pan over low heat until fragrant.

Transfer the roasted spices to a spice grinder or pestle and mortar and grind to a powder. Add the remaining ingredients and grind together. Store in an airtight container.

MAKES 125 G (5 OZ/$\frac{1}{2}$ CUP)

Ka-Thi

Coconut Milk and Cream

Grated coconut is best when it is fresh. Dried or desiccated coconut can also be used to make coconut milk but it needs to be soaked, then chopped more finely or ground to a paste, otherwise it will be fibrous. If you can, buy a proper coconut grater.

1 coconut (yields about 300 g/11 oz flesh)

Drain the coconut by punching a hole in two of the dark, coloured eyes. Drain out the liquid and use it as a refreshing drink. Holding the coconut in one hand, tap around the circumference firmly with a hammer or pestle. This should cause the coconut to split open evenly. (If it doesn't crack easily, put it in a 150°C/300°F/Gas 2 oven for 15 minutes. This may cause it to crack as it cools. If it doesn't, it will crack easily when hit with a hammer.)

If you would like to use a coconut grater, the easiest ones to use are the ones that you sit at one end, then scrape out the coconut from each half on the serrated edge, catching the grated coconut meat in a large bowl. If you don't have a coconut grater, prise the flesh out of the shell, trim off the hard, brown, outer skin and grate either by hand on a box grater or chop in a food processor. Grated coconut can be frozen in small portions until it is needed.

Mix the grated coconut with 125 ml (4 fl oz/½ cup) hot water and leave to steep for 5 minutes. Pour the mixture into a container through a sieve lined with muslin, then gather the muslin into a ball to squeeze out any remaining liquid. This will make a thick coconut milk, which is usually called coconut cream.

Repeat the steeping and squeezing process with another 250 ml (9 fl oz/1 cup) of water to make thinner coconut milk.

MAKES 125 ML (4 FL OZ/½ CUP) COCONUT CREAM AND 250 ML (9 FL OZ/1 CUP) COCONUT MILK

Khao Plao

Steamed Rice

400 g (14 oz/2 cups) jasmine rice

Rinse the rice until the water runs clear. Put the rice in a saucepan and add enough water to come an index-finger joint above the rice. Bring to the boil, then cover and cook at a slow simmer for 10–15 minutes. Remove from the heat and leave it to rest for 10 minutes.

SERVES 4

Khao Niaw

Sticky Rice

400 g (14 oz/2 cups) sticky rice

Put the rice in a bowl and pour in cold water to come 5 cm (2 in) above the rice. Soak for at least 3 hours, or overnight. Drain and transfer to a bamboo basket specially made for steaming sticky rice, or to a steamer lined with a double thickness of muslin. Spread the rice in the steamer. Bring the water in the bottom of the steamer to a rolling boil. Taking care, set the rice over the water. Lower the heat, cover and steam for 20–25 minutes, or until the rice swells and is glistening and tender. The cooking time will vary depending on the soaking time. Check and replenish the water every 10 minutes or so.

When the rice is cooked, tip it onto a large tray and spread it out to help it cool quickly. If it cools slowly it will be soggy rather than sticky. Serve warm or cold.

SERVES 4

Khao Niaw Ka-Thi
Steamed Sticky Rice with Coconut Milk

200 g (7 oz/1 cup) sticky rice
170 ml (6 fl oz/^{2}/$_3$ cup) coconut milk (page 245),
    well stirred

1 tablespoon palm sugar (jaggery)
^{1}/$_2$ teaspoon salt

Rinse the rice until the water runs clear. Put the rice in a saucepan and add enough water to come an index-finger joint above the rice. Bring to the boil, then cover and cook at a slow simmer for 10–15 minutes. Remove from the heat and leave it to rest for 10 minutes.

SERVES 4

Khai Kem
Salted Eggs

10 fresh duck eggs (if available), or large chicken eggs,
    cleaned

175 g (6 oz) salt

Being very careful not to crack the shells, place the eggs into a preserving jar large enough to hold all the eggs.

In a saucepan, heat 625 ml (22 fl oz/2^1/$_2$ cups) of water and the salt until the salt has dissolved. Allow to cool.

Pour the cool salt water into the preserving jar with the eggs. Seal the jar and leave for only three weeks. If you leave them any longer they will get too salty. Salted eggs will last for up to two months in the jar. Drain and use as required: boil the eggs, then scoop out the yolks and discard the whites.

MAKES 10

GLOSSARY

ASIAN SHALLOTS (hawn)
Small reddish-purple shallots used in Southeast Asia. French shallots can be used instead.

BAMBOO SHOOTS (naw mai)
The edible shoots of bamboo. Available fresh in season, otherwise preserved in jars or canned. Fresh shoots should be blanched if bitter.

BANANA FLOWER (hua plii) or blossom
This is the purple, teardrop-shaped flower of the banana plant. The purple leaves and pale yellow buds that grow between them are discarded. Only the inner pale core is eaten and this needs to be blanched in boiling water to remove any bitterness. It is advisable to wear rubber gloves to prepare banana flower as it has a gummy substance that can stain your fingers. Shredded banana flowers appear in salads and sometimes in curries.

BANANA LEAVES (bai tawng)
Large green leaves, which can be used as a wrapping (dip briefly in boiling water or put in a hot oven for 10 seconds to soften) for foods, or to line plates. Young leaves are preferable.

BANANAS (kluay)
There are more than 20 different types of banana available in Thailand, all of which are used in cooking and are very popular.

BASIL
There are three types of basil used in Thai cuisine. Thai sweet basil (bai horapha) is the most common. This has purplish stems, green leaves and an aniseed aroma and flavour. It is aromatic and is used in curries, soups and stir-fries. Holy basil (bai ka-phrao) is either red or green with slightly pointed, variegated leaves. Holy basil is used in stir-fries and fish dishes. Lemon basil (bai maeng-lak) is also called mint basil. It is less common and is used in curries and stir-fries.

BETEL LEAVES (bai cha-phluu)
Known also as piper leaves or wild tea leaves, these are not true betel but are a close relative. They are used to wrap some snacks. Use baby spinach leaves if you can't get betel leaves.

BLACK FUNGUS
A funghi that is available fresh and dried, this has a cartilaginous texture and very little flavour. It is used in Chinese-style soups and stir-fries.

CARDAMOM (luuk kra-waan)
A round white variety of cardamom is used in Indian- or Muslim-influenced curries such as massaman. Common green cardamom can be used instead. Use the pods whole or crushed.

CHA OM
A bitter green vegetable resembling a fern, used in omelette-style dishes and in stir-fries.

CHILLI JAM (naam jim phrik)
A thick, sweet chilli relish that can also be used as a sauce.

CHILLI SAUCE
The common name for siracha chilli sauce (naam phrik sii raachaa), this is used more than any of the many other types of chilli sauce. Usually

served alongside grilled fish, this thick orange sauce is named after the seaside town famous for its production. Chilli sauce goes with anything.

CHILLIES (phrik)
Red and green chillies are widely used in Thai cuisine. Recipes usually give a variety, rather than a colour. Generally, with Thai chillies, the smaller they are the hotter they are. Bird's eye or mouse dropping chillies (phrik khii nuu) are the smallest and hottest. Most commonly green, but red can be used in most recipes. Dragon's eye chillies (phrik khii nuu suan) are slightly larger and less hot. Sky-pointing or long chillies (phrik chii faa) are about 5 cm (2 in) long and milder than the smaller ones. Used in stir-fries, salads and curry pastes. Orange chillies (phrik leuang) are hot but not as hot as bird's eye chillies. Banana chillies (phrik yuak) are large fat yellow/green chillies with a mild flavour. They are used in stir-fries as well as in salads. Dried red chillies (phrik haeng) are either long chillies or bird's eye. They are sometimes softened in hot water. Remove the seeds if you prefer less heat.

CHINESE KALE (phak kaa-naa)
Known as gai laan in Chinese food shops.

CHINESE KEYS (kra-chai)
A rhizome with skinny fingers that hang down like a bunch of keys. Has a peppery flavour. Available tinned, or preserved in jars.

COCONUT (maphrao)
The fruit of a coconut palm. The inner nut is encased in a husk which has to be removed. The hard shell can then be drained of juice before being cracked open to extract the white meat. Coconut meat is jellyish in younger nuts and harder in older ones. Medium-hard coconuts, which are perfect for desserts, are sold as grating coconuts in Thailand.

COCONUT CREAM (hua ka-thi)
This is made by soaking freshly grated coconut in boiling water and then squeezing out a thick, sweet coconut-flavoured liquid. It is available tinned but if you want to make your own, see page 245

COCONUT MILK (haang ka-thi)
A thinner version of coconut cream, made as above but with more water or from a second pressing. Available tinned, but to make your own, see page 245.

COCONUT SUGAR (naamtaan maphrao)
This sugar is made from the sap from coconut trees. Dark brown in colour, it is mainly used in sweet dishes. Palm sugar (jaggery) or unrefined soft brown sugar can be used instead.

CORIANDER (phak chii)
Coriander leaves are used as an ingredient and as a garnish. The roots (raak phak chii) are chopped or ground and used in curry pastes and sauces.

CURRY PASTES (khreuang kaeng)
Most often homemade in Thailand, though they can be bought freshly made in markets, and packaged in supermarkets. All curry pastes are ground and pounded together in a pestle and mortar until they are very smooth.

CURRY POWDER (phong karii)
Usually bought ready-made in Thailand as it is not widely used.

DRIED FISH (plaa haeng)
Used extensively in Thai cuisine, dried fish is usually fried and crumbled and used in dips, salads and pastes.

DRIED SHRIMP (kung haeng)
These are either ground until they form a fine fluff or rehydrated and used whole. Look for dark pink ones.

DURIAN (thurian)
The most infamous of fruit with a notoriously noxious aroma and sweet, creamy flavour and texture. It is banned from airlines and hotels.

EGGPLANT (makheua)

There are lots of varieties of eggplant (aubergine) used in Thai cuisine and, unlike in the West, bitterness is a prized quality. Common eggplants include Thai eggplant (ma-kheua phraw) which are pale green, orange, purple, yellow or white and golf-ball sized. Long eggplant (ma-kheua yao) are long, skinny and green. Pea eggplant (ma-kheua phuang) are tiny, bitter and look like large peas. Cut eggplant using a stainless steel knife and store in salted water to prevent them from turning black.

FISH SAUCE (naam plaa)

Made from salted anchovy-like fish that are left to break down naturally in the heat, fish sauce is literally the liquid that is drained off. It is the main source of salt flavouring in Thai cooking and is also used as a condiment. A fermented version (naam plaa raa) is used in the north and north-east of Thailand.

GALANGAL/GALINGALE (khaa)

A rhizome, similar to ginger, used extensively in Thai cooking, usually in place of ginger. It is most famously used in tom khaa kai.

GARLIC (kra-tiam)

Thai garlic has tiny cloves and is usually smashed with the side of a cleaver rather than being crushed. Deep-fried garlic is used as a garnish as is garlic oil.

JACKFRUIT (kha-nun)

A large spiky fruit with segmented flesh enclosing large stones. It tastes like fruit salad and is used unripe in curries.

KETCHAP MANIS

A thick, sweet soy sauce used as a flavouring.

LEMON GRASS (ta-khrai)

Used in many Thai dishes. The fibrous stalk of a citrus perfumed grass, it is finely chopped or sliced or cut into chunks. Discard the outer layers until you reach a softer purple layer.

LIMES (ma-nao)

Limes and lime juice are used extensively in Thai cuisine. Lime juice is a souring agent though Thai limes are sweeter than their Western counterparts.

LYCHEES (linchii)

Small round fruit with a red leathery skin and translucent white flesh surrounding a brown stone. Very perfumed and often available peeled and seeded in a syrup as a dessert.

MAKRUT (KAFFIR) LIMES (luk makrut)

These knobbly skinned fruit are used for their zest. Leaves (bai makrut) are double leaves with a fragrant citrus oil. They are used very finely shredded or torn into large pieces.

MANGOES (ma-muang)

Green unripe mangoes are used in relishes, curries, soups and salads, or preserved in brine. Ripe mangoes are eaten out of the hand or alongside sticky rice as a dessert.

MINT (sa-ra-nae)

Mint is used in salads such as laap as well as being served alongside salads and noodle soups.

MUNG BEAN SPROUTS (thua ngawk)

These are used in stir-fries, soups and salads. Store in a bowl of cold water in the fridge.

MUNG BEANS (thua leuang)

Whole beans are puréed or ground and used in desserts. Also used to make a type of noodle.

NOODLES

Rice noodles (kuaytiaw) are made of rice flour and water and steamed in sheets before being cut into widths. Wide line or sen yai noodles are about 2.5 cm (1 in) wide, small line (sen lek) are 5 mm (¼ in) in width and line noodles (sen mii) are 1–2 mm. Rice noodles are sold fresh and dried. The widths can be used interchangeably. Wheat noodles (ba-mii) are usually made with egg. Mung bean starch noodles (wun sen) are very thin white translucent noodles that go clear when soaked. Both wun sen and sen mii are referred to as vermicelli.

OYSTER SAUCE
Use the Thai version of the Chinese sauce if you can. It has a stronger oyster flavour.

PALM SUGAR (JAGGERY) (naamtaan piip)
Palm sugar is made by boiling sugar palm sap until it turns into a granular paste. Sold in hard cakes or as a slightly softer version in tubs. Malaysian and Indonesian palm sugar are darker in colour and stronger in flavour. Unrefined, soft light brown sugar can be used instead.

PANDANUS LEAVES (bai toey)
These long green leaves are shaped like blades and are used as a flavouring in desserts and sweets, as well as a wrapping for small parcels of food. Essence can be bought in small bottles from speciality Asian food shops. Pandanus leaves are often sold frozen.

PEANUTS (thua lisong)
Peanuts are used raw in curries, deep-fried as a garnish, or in dipping sauces. Buy raw peanuts and fry them yourself for the best results.

PEPPERCORNS (phrik thai)
Green peppercorns are used fresh in curries. Dried white peppercorns are used as a seasoning and as a garnish but black pepper is seldom used.

PICKLED GARLIC (kra-tiam dong)
Eaten as an accompaniment, pickled garlic has a sweet/sour flavour. Preserved as whole heads that can be used as they are.

PICKLED GINGER (khing dong)
Used as an accompaniment to curries and snacks.

PRESERVED CABBAGE (phak gaund dong)
Salted and preserved cabbage is usually sold shredded. It sometimes comes in earthenware pots and is labelled Tianjin preserved vegetables.

PRESERVED PLUMS
Salty, sour, preserved plums are used in sweet/sour dishes, to make plum sauce, and with steamed fish.

PRESERVED RADISH (tang chai)
Salted and preserved radish is sold shredded or as strips. It is also referred to by the Japanese name, daikon, or the Indian, mooli. Comes salty and sweet/salty.

RAMBUTAN (ngaw)
A small round fruit with a red skin covered in soft, fine red spikes. Buy rambutan when they are vibrant in colour.

RICE (khao)
Jasmine (long-grain) and sticky rice are the two main varieties eaten in Thailand. Sticky rice comes in white and black, which is quite purple in reality. Jasmine rice is steamed, boiled or, more traditionally, cooked in a clay pot. Sticky rice is soaked and then steamed, either in a steamer or packed into lengths of bamboo.

RICE FLOUR (paeng khao)
Made from white and black rice, this is also known as ground rice and is used in desserts.

ROASTED CHILLI POWDER (phrik bon)
Both bird's eye and sky-pointing chillies are used to make chilli powder. Buy or make your own by roasting and grinding whole chillies.

ROASTED CHILLI SAUCE (naam phrik phao)
This sauce is made from dried red chillies roasted in oil. It usually includes shrimp paste and palm sugar. Roasted chilli sauce comes in mild, medium and hot and is sold in jars and plastic pouches. To make your own, see page 240. Use as a flavouring and as a relish.

ROSE APPLE (chom-phuu)
A crisp, watery fruit with no overwhelming taste, except for sweetness. Eaten on its own and sometimes as an accompaniment to dips.

SAGO (saku)

Small dried balls of sago palm sap, which are used for milky desserts and savoury dishes. Cooked sago is transparent and soft with a silky texture.

SHRIMP PASTE (ka-pi)

A strong smelling dark brownish-pink paste sold in small tubs that are usually sealed with wax. It is made from salted, fermented and dried shrimp. Buy a Thai version as those from other Asian countries vary. This is very strong smelling and is an ingredient in dips such as naam phrik.

SNAKE BEANS (thua fak yao)

Also called long beans or yard-long beans, these are sold in coils or tied together in bunches. Eaten fresh and cooked. Green beans can be used instead.

SOUR SAUSAGE

Thai sausages can be bought ready-made or you can make them yourself (see page 43). They sometimes come wrapped in cellophane or banana leaves, or are strung together. Chinese sausages can be used instead.

SOY SAUCE (sii-yu)

Both light soy sauce (sii-yu khao) and dark soy (sii-yu dam) are used in Thai cooking. The dark one is sweeter than Chinese-style soy sauce.

SPRING ROLL SHEETS

Wheat and egg dough wrappers that can be bought from Asian food shops and some good supermarkets. Look in the refrigerator or freezer sections. Squares of filo can also be used.

TAMARIND (ma-khaam)

A fruit whose flesh is used as a souring agent. Usually bought as a dried cake or prepared as a purée, tamarind is actually a pod filled with seeds and a fibrous flesh. If you buy tamarind cake, it must be soaked in hot water and then rubbed and squeezed to dissolve the pulp around the fibres. The fibres are then sieved out. Pulp is sold as purée or concentrate but is sometimes referred to as tamarind water. Freshly made tamarind water has a fresher, stronger flavour.

TAPIOCA FLOUR

Made from ground, dried cassava root, this flour is used in desserts, dumpling wrappers and as a thickener.

TOFU (tao-huu)

Also known as bean curd, this can be firm or silken (soft).

TURMERIC (kha-min)

A rhizome like ginger and galangal. In Thailand turmeric comes in white and yellow varieties. The yellow type is often referred to as red and is used fresh in curry pastes. Dried, it adds a yellow colour to curries. The white type is often eaten raw as an accompaniment to naam phrik.

VINEGAR (naam som)

White coconut vinegar is the most common. Any mild white vinegar or better still, rice vinegar, can be used as a substitute.

WATER SPINACH (phak bung)

Also called kang kong, morning glory, ong choy and water convolvulus, this is a leafy green vegetable that has hollow stems. Used as an ingredient as well as an accompaniment.

WING BEANS (thua phuu)

Also called angle beans, these have four frilly edges. Used cut into cross sections in salads and stir-fries. Buy as fresh as you can.

WON TON SHEETS

These sheets or wrappers are available from the refrigerator or freezer cabinets of Asian food shops. Some are yellow and include egg in the pastry and others are white.

YELLOW BEAN SAUCE (tao jiaw)

This paste made of yellow soy beans adds a salty flavour to dishes.

Index

B

bamboo shoots 248
bananas 248
    banana in coconut
      cream 227
    banana flower 248
    banana leaves 248
    deep-fried bananas
      232
    snapper with green
      banana and mango
      147
barbecued pork spare ribs
  118
basil 248
beans
    beef with black bean
      sauce 163
    fried fish cakes with
      green beans 34
    pork with snake beans
      163
    stir-fried snake beans
      215
    wing bean salad 211
beef
    beef with black bean
      sauce 163
    beef with Thai sweet
      basil leaves 162
    dried beef 115
    massaman curry with
      beef 149
    panaeng beef curry
      128
    sliced steak with hot
      and sour sauce 73
betel leaves 248
    with savoury topping
      20
black fungus 248
broccoli, stir-fried with oyster
  sauce 210

C

cabbage, preserved 251
caramel pork 122
cardamom 248
cha om 248
Chiang Mai curry paste 237
Chiang Mai noodles 193
Chiang Mai pork curry 133
chicken
    betel leaves with
      savoury topping 20
    Chiang Mai noodles
      193
    chicken with cashew
      nuts 168
    chicken with chilli jam
      162
    chicken, coconut and
      galangal soup 64
    chicken with crispy holy
      basil leaves 160
    chicken and papaya
      salad 70
    chicken satay 27
    chicken wrapped in
      pandanus leaf 45
    curry puffs 29
    gold bags 16
    green curry with chicken
      131
    grilled chicken 112
    rice soup with prawns
      and chicken 65
    spring rolls 21
    vegetable soup with
      chicken and prawns
      54
    yellow chicken curry
      with peppercorns 150
chillies 249
    chicken with chilli jam
      162
    chilli jam 240, 248

chilli sauce 248
    curried fish steamed in
      banana chillies 93
    deep-fried fish with
      chillies and basil 90
    fried rice with prawns
      and chilli jam 185
    garlic and chilli sauce
      241
    mixed seafood with
      chillies 156
    prawns with coriander
      leaves and chilli 43
    pumpkin with chilli and
      basil 214
    roast chilli sauce 240,
      251
    roasted chilli powder
      251
    sweet chilli sauce 241
Chinese kale 249
Chinese keys 249
clams and mussels with
  Chinese keys 94
coconut 249
    banana in coconut
      cream 227
    chicken, coconut and
      galangal soup 64
    coconut cream 245,
      249
    coconut ice cream
      226
    coconut milk 245, 249
    coconut sugar 249
    steamed sticky rice with
      coconut milk 247
    sticky rice with shrimp or
      coconut topping 37
    tapioca pudding with
      young coconut 227
coriander 249
corn cakes, sweet 28

crab
    crab and green mango
      salad 76
    cracked crab with curry
      powder 102
crisp rubies 220
cucumber relish 243
curry
    Chiang Mai pork curry
      133
    cracked crab with curry
      powder 102
    curried fish steamed in
      banana chillies 93
    curry puffs 29
    green curry with chicken
      131
    green curry with fish
      balls 140
    jungle curry with prawns
      132
    massaman curry with
      beef 149
    panaeng beef curry
      128
    prawns with Thai sweet
      basil leaves 133
    red curry with roasted
      duck and lychees 146
    red pork curry with green
      peppercorns 136
    snapper with green
      banana and mango
      147
    spicy lobster and
      pineapple curry 139
    yellow chicken curry
      with peppercorns 150
curry pastes 236–8, 249
curry powder 243, 249
custards 224
    pumpkin with custard
      233

D

dipping sauces
  shrimp paste dipping sauce 208
  spicy tomato dipping sauce 204
dry curry paste 237
duck
  red curry with roasted duck and lychees 146
  spicy ground duck 77
durian 249

E

egg noodles with seafood 198
eggplant 250
  baby eggplant and cherry tomato stir-fry 215
eggs
  salted eggs 247
  son-in-law eggs 24

F

fish
  crispy fish salad 83
  curried fish steamed in banana chillies 93
  deep-fried fish with chillies and basil 90
  deep-fried fish with three-flavoured sauce 104
  dried fish 249
  fish sauce 250
  fish steamed in banana leaf 107
  fried fish cakes with green beans 34
  green curry with fish balls 140
  grilled fish with garlic and coriander 101
  hot and sour grilled fish salad 76
  rice soup with fish fillets 57
  snapper with green banana and mango 147

sour fish soup with water spinach 57
steamed fish with preserved plum 105
fragrant tofu and tomato soup 50
fried rice with pineapple 181
fried rice with prawns and chilli jam 185

G

galangal 250
galloping horses 20
garlic 250
  garlic and chilli sauce 241
  grilled fish with garlic and coriander 101
  pickled garlic 251
  pork with garlic and pepper 173
  stir-fried garlic prawns 172
ginger, pickled 251
ginger, pork with 167
gold bags 16
green curry paste 238
green papaya salad 42

H

hot and sour grilled fish salad 76
hot and sour noodles with prawns 185
hot and sour prawn soup 53
hot and sour vermicelli with mixed seafood 84

I

ice cream, coconut 226

J

jackfruit 250
jungle curry with prawns 132

K

ketchap manis 250

L

lemon grass 250
limes 250
lychees 250

M

makrut limes 250
mangoes 250
  crab and green mango salad 76
  mango sorbet 232
  snapper with green banana and mango 147
  sticky rice with mango 226
massaman curry with beef 149
massaman curry paste 236
mint 250
mung bean sprouts 250
mung beans 250
mushrooms with tofu 159
mussels
  clams and mussels with Chinese keys 94
  fried mussel pancake 40
  mussels with lemon grass 94

N

noodles 250
  Chiang Mai noodles 193
  crispy rice noodles 199
  egg noodles with seafood 198
  hot and sour noodles with prawns 185
  stir-fried egg noodles with vegetables 184
  stir-fried noodles with holy basil 184
  stir-fried white noodles with pork 190
  Thai fried noodles with prawns 178

O

oyster sauce 251

P

palm sugar 251
panaeng beef curry 128
pancake, fried mussel 40
pandanus leaves 251
papaya
  chicken and papaya salad 70
  green papaya salad 42
peanut sauce 242
peanuts 251
peppercorns 251
plum sauce 242
plums, preserved 251
pork
  barbecued pork spare ribs 118
  betel leaves with savoury topping 20
  braised pork 115
  caramel pork 122
  Chiang Mai pork curry 133
  curry puffs 29
  deep-fried pork spare ribs 118
  galloping horses 20
  gold bags 16
  pork with garlic and pepper 173
  pork with ginger 167
  pork sausages 43
  pork with snake beans 163
  pork on sticks 116
  pork with sweet and sour sauce 171
  red pork curry with green peppercorns 136
  spring rolls 21
  stir-fried white noodles with pork 190
  vermicelli soup with minced pork 61
prawns
  curry puffs 29
  fried rice with prawns and chilli jam 185
  gold bags 16
  hot and sour noodles with prawns 185
  hot and sour prawn soup 53

jungle curry with prawns 132

prawn and pomelo salad 74

prawns in a blanket 19

prawns with coriander leaves and chilli 43

prawns and sausage in a clay pot 189

prawns with Thai sweet basil leaves 133

rice soup with prawns and chicken 65

sesame prawns on toasts 28

sticky rice with shrimp or coconut topping 37

stir-fried garlic prawns 172

stuffed tofu soup with prawns 56

Thai fried noodles with prawns 178

vegetable soup with chicken and prawns 54

won ton soup with prawns 182

pumpkin with chilli and basil 214

pumpkin with custard 233

Q

quail, deep-fried 119

R

radish, preserved 251

rambutan 251

red curry paste 236

rice 251

black sticky rice with taro 223

fried rice with pineapple 181

fried rice with prawns and chilli jam 185

prawns and sausage in a clay pot 189

rice flour 251

rice soup with fish fillets 57

rice soup with prawns and chicken 65

steamed rice 246

steamed sticky rice with coconut milk 247

sticky rice 246

sticky rice with mango 226

sticky rice with shrimp or coconut topping 37

rose apple 251

S

sago 252

salads

chicken and papaya salad 70

crab and green mango salad 76

crispy fish salad 83

green papaya salad 42

hot and sour grilled fish salad 76

hot and sour vermicelli with mixed seafood 84

prawn and pomelo salad 74

sliced steak with hot and sour sauce 73

wing bean salad 211

salted eggs 247

satay, chicken 27

sauces 240–2

sausages

pork sausages 43

prawns and sausage in a clay pot 189

sour sausage 252

seafood

egg noodles with seafood 198

hot and sour vermicelli with mixed seafood 84

mixed seafood with chillies 156

spicy lobster and pineapple curry 139

stuffed squid soup 62

see also crab; fish; mussels; prawns

sesame prawns on toasts 28

shallots, Asian 248

shrimp

dried shrimp 249

shrimp paste 252

shrimp paste dipping sauce 208

see also prawns

snake beans 252

stir-fried 215

snapper with green banana and mango 147

son-in-law eggs 24

sorbet, mango 232

soup

chicken, coconut and galangal soup 64

fragrant tofu and tomato soup 50

hot and sour prawn soup 53

rice soup with fish fillets 57

rice soup with prawns and chicken 65

sour fish soup with water spinach 57

stuffed squid soup 62

stuffed tofu soup with prawns 56

vegetable soup with chicken and prawns 54

vermicelli soup with minced pork 61

won ton soup with prawns 182

sour fish soup with water spinach 57

soy sauce 252

spring roll sheets 252

spring rolls 21

sticky rice 246

black sticky rice with taro 223

steamed sticky rice with coconut milk 247

sticky rice with mango 226

sticky rice with shrimp or coconut topping 37

sweet chilli sauce 241

sweet corn cakes 28

sesame prawns on toasts 28

shallots, Asian 248

T

tamarind 252

tapioca flour 252

tapioca pudding with young coconut 227

taro, black sticky rice with 223

tofu 252

fragrant tofu and tomato soup 50

mushrooms with tofu 159

stuffed tofu soup with prawns 56

tomatoes

baby eggplant and cherry tomato stir-fry 215

fragrant tofu and tomato soup 50

spicy tomato dipping sauce 204

turmeric 252

V

vegetables

stir-fried mixed vegetables 207

vegetable soup with chicken and prawns 54

vermicelli soup with minced pork 61

vinegar 252

W

water spinach 252

stir-fried 210

wing bean salad 211

wing beans 252

won ton sheets 252

won ton soup with prawns 182

Y

yellow bean sauce 252

yellow curry paste 238

Published in 2010 by Murdoch Books Pty Limited

Murdoch Books Australia
Pier 8/9, 23 Hickson Road
Millers Point NSW 2000
Phone: +61 (0)2 8220 2000
Fax: +61 (0)2 8220 2558
www.murdochbooks.com.au

Murdoch Books UK Limited
Erico House, 6th Floor
93–99 Upper Richmond Road
Putney, London SW15 2TG
Phone: +44 (0)20 8785 5995
Fax: +44 (0)20 8785 5985
www.murdochbooks.co.uk

Publisher: Lynn Lewis
Senior Designer: Heather Menzies
Series Design Concept: Sarah Odgers
Photographer: Alan Benson, Natasha Milne, Ashley Mackevicus,
Prue Roscoe, Ian Hofsetter and Martin Brigdale
Project Editor: Justine Harding
Designer: Susanne Geppert
Index: Jo Rudd

Text copyright © 2010 Murdoch Books
The moral right of the author has been asserted.
Design copyright © Murdoch Books Pty Limited 2010
Photography copyright © Alan Benson, Natasha Milne, Ashley Mackevicus,
Prue Roscoe, Ian Hofsetter and Martin Brigdale

All rights reserved. No part of this publication may be reproduced, stored in a retrieval system or transmitted in any form or by any means, electronic, mechanical, photocopying, recording or otherwise, without the prior written permission of the publisher.

ISBN: 978-1-74266-105-6

PRINTED IN CHINA.

IMPORTANT: Those who might be at risk from the effects of salmonella poisoning (the elderly, pregnant women, young children and those suffering from immune deficiency diseases) should consult their doctor with any concerns about eating raw eggs.

OVEN GUIDE: You may find cooking times vary depending on the oven you are using. For fan-forced ovens, as a general rule, set the oven temperature to 20°C (35°F) lower than indicated in the recipe.